KU-325-532

DISPOSED OF
BY LIBRARY
HOUSE OF LORDS

INNOVATIONS IN POLICING

INNOVATIONS IN POLICING

Mollie Weatheritt

CROOM HELM
London ● Sydney ● Dover, New Hampshire

In association with
THE POLICE FOUNDATION

© 1986 Mollie Weatheritt
Croom Helm Ltd, Provident House, Burrell Row,
Beckenham, Kent BR3 1AT
Croom Helm Australia Pty Ltd, Suite 4, 6th Floor,
64–76 Kippax Street, Surry Hills, NSW 2010, Australia

British Library Cataloguing in Publication Data

Weatheritt, Mollie.
  Innovations in policing.
    1. Police–England.
    I. Title.
    363-2'0942   HV8196.A2
    ISBN 0-7099-4044-0

Croom Helm, 51 Washington St, Dover
New Hampshire 03820, USA

Library of Congress Cataloging in Publication Data

Weatheritt, Mollie
  Innovations in Policing.

    Bibliography: p.
    1. Police — Great Britain. 2. Police — Great Britain —
Attitudes. 3. Crime Prevention — Great Britain.
I. Title.
HV8195.A3W42 1986   363.2'0941   85-29130
ISBN 0-7099-4044-0

Filmset by Mayhew Typesetting, Bristol, England
Printed and bound in Great Britain by Mackays of Chatham Ltd, Kent

CONTENTS

Foreword

Acknowledgements

FOREWORD

Policing reflects society and changes with it. Change is thus hardly new to the police — in 1857 the reports of Her Majesty's Inspectors of Constabulary were already suggesting changes to forces established by the County and Borough Police Act only the year before.

What is new, however, is the pace of change. This has been particularly rapid over the past decade and is still increasing. It is as much this very rate of change as change itself which causes problems for those involved in planning and managing for the future.

The rate of change has led to the development of a much more questioning approach by the police service to what it does. Long held assumptions are coming under detailed scrutiny and there is a growing interest in developing measurable indicators of police performance to replace what has hitherto often been the subjective impressions of those most closely involved. The development of such indicators is not easy. Unlike manufacturing industries, the police service has no identifiable end product, nor do its customers — who range from central and local government to community groups and individuals — all agree on what they want from the police. Defining objectives for the police service against which performance might be measured is correspondingly difficult, and even where this is possible it is often difficult for the police to achieve these objectives. The police service has to aim for an equilibrium: a balance between the demands and needs of its various customers and what it is possible to provide within the limits of its resources.

Mollie Weatheritt sets out to describe some of the attempts the police service has made to come to grips with the re-evaluation of its activities that it is now undertaking. She makes no pretence at comprehensiveness. Her purpose is rather to provide illustrations of the sorts of pitfalls that police evaluators need to avoid and some of the problems they may encounter. Her message is that particular innovations must be examined in their context and that no innovation or technique should be seen as a panacea for any and every problem. She identifies some of the difficulties associated with once and for all change and suggests how systems of monitoring and review may ease the path of change and make it less traumatic.

It is one of the inevitable drawbacks of the kind of review that Mollie Weatheritt has undertaken that by the time it is published, events have

Foreword

moved on. Some of the earlier studies described in this book have already been replicated and hence validated or rejected while many more policing initiatives will have been established. This book nonetheless provides a good basis for continuing assessment and for developing further reviews. I feel it will stimulate discussion inside and outside the police service and will help us to learn a little more about ourselves and our place in society.

Stanley Bailey
Chief Constable of Northumbria
President, Association of Chief Police Officers

ACKNOWLEDGEMENTS

Like many books, this one owes a lot to the time, effort and patience of others too numerous to mention individually. I am especially grateful to the many police officers of all ranks who provided me with a great deal of factual information and the opportunity to talk through some of the ideas expressed here. Not all of them will agree with the result. I can only hope that they will feel that it is not too great a travesty of what they would recognise to be the case.

I am also grateful to past and present colleagues in the Police Foundation and in the Home Office who commented on earlier drafts, corrected errors and helped me clarify some of my ideas. The errors and opacities that remain are of course entirely my responsibility. I am especially indebted to Barrie Irving and Andrew Crook for sustaining me in the belief that the enterprise was worthwhile: at times this must have seemed a very heavy burden to bear.

A modified version of Chapter 2 originally appeared in *Policing*. I am grateful to the Police Review Publishing Co for permission to reproduce it.

Mollie Weatheritt
Police Foundation

1 SETTING THE SCENE

This book is the result of a review that the Police Foundation asked me to prepare of innovation and experiment in the police service. The review was to have two main aims. One was to try to show how the police are responding to changing demands and pressures on them and the extent to which they are open-minded and receptive to change. The second aim was to disseminate to a wider public information which is currently not readily accessible to it; and to provide a basis for cross-fertilisation of ideas within the service itself. The Foundation felt that there was a great deal going on in forces that could act as a spur to innovation and change in others, if it was consistently documented and made more widely known.

I was given a free hand in determining the nature and boundaries of the review. It soon became clear that it would be an enormous task to document all those aspects of organisational structure, function and philosophy where the service has recently considered the possibilities for change or is working towards it. Modern police forces are large and complex organisations, expected to perform a diversity of functions and tasks using an increasingly complex set of methods and techniques and under pressure to account for their activities in ways which satisfy a variety of constituencies. Rather than try to document all these activities, I chose to concentrate on two main aspects of them. The first concerns those ways in which the police seek to legitimate their own activity by emphasising the consensual rather than the conflictual aspects of policing — its socially integrative functions at the expense of its potentially divisive ones, and its preventive as opposed to its enforcement face. In other words, although I have avoided using the term, I look at what have become widely known as 'community policing' initiatives in their various guises and how these translate into practical activity of different kinds. In practice I cover two main sorts of initiatives: how the police deploy manpower, particularly on patrol, and new departures in crime prevention which involve the police in planning and acting in collaboration with other agencies to reduce the opportunities or motivation to commit crime.

The second aspect of policing I concentrate on relates less to practical activity than to the approach the police adopt to defining problems and devising solutions to them and their willingness and ability to look critically at the results of their own activity and to draw lessons from them. In common with the other public services, the police are under

1

pressure from the squeeze on public expenditure to show that they do their job effectively and organise themselves efficiently — in other words, that they give value for money. I therefore devote considerable space to how the police account for what they do in terms of its efficiency and its effectiveness; and what the implications of these twin ideas are for programmes of innovation and change.

A great deal however, is omitted from this review. Although much of what I describe bears on issues of accountability, I have not examined the formal structures through which the police are accountable. Thus I have not looked at the changing role of police authorities, nor the growth, especially in London, of borough police committees and police monitoring groups. Nor have I tried to document the kinds of police-community liaison structures envisaged in the Scarman report and given statutory effect by the Police and Criminal Evidence Act 1984. My concern has been more with the operational aspects of policing and the ways in which the police justify that activity themselves. The form those justifications take are in my view as important for understanding issues of accountability as any formal structures. They have far-reaching implications for the wider context in which policing issues get presented and discussed.

Nor have I looked at training. Two reviews — one on probationer training and one on race relations training — were published while this review was in preparation (Home Office, 1983a, b). Both summarise the state of the art and both make recommendations designed to improve on what is currently being offered: probationer training for example will continue to be subject to detailed review (see *Police*, 1984). It seemed superfluous for me to go over the same ground.

A third omission is in the area of police procedure. I have not looked, for example, at new ways the police have devised for dealing with juvenile offenders, such as instant cautioning schemes,[1] nor at other aspects of prosecution policy and procedure such as initiatives in many forces to reduce the number and types of prosecutions for traffic offences (see, for example, Dix and Layzell, 1983, p. 64). I assumed that, because the boundaries within which the police can properly act are more tightly drawn by law, custom and practice than those in which other public services perform their tasks, police scope for experimenting with new ideas would be correspondingly limited. For this reason, innovations seemed likely to be thin on the ground and I therefore decided to omit them altogether. As it happened, two potentially important innovations were introduced on an experimental basis during the period of the review: the tape-recording of police interviews with suspects (Willis, 1984) and lay visitors to police stations (*Police Review*, 1983; Community/Police Consultative Group for Lambeth, 1984). Perhaps the most significant omission from the review is any extended discussion of the place of technology in policing. Many scientific and technological developments are of limited interest except to a small circle of specialists (see, for example, the annual reports of the Home Office Central Research Establishment and the annual research and development programme of the Home Office Scientific Research and Development Branch; also Manwaring-White, 1984, Ch. 7). None the less, technical research and development absorbs a large proportion of the government funds available for police research (see Chapter 2) and the impact of apparently neutral technical developments can be considerable, both on the way the police are viewed and on the kinds of service they offer. The introduction of panda cars and personal radios in the 1960s is a frequently cited example of how two apparently straightforward innovations have had social consequences far beyond those originally intended or envisaged for them (see Chapter 6).

To do justice to the actual and potential impact of technical change on the nature and consequences of policing would take a book in itself. It is a subject that remains virtually untouched by research. There is a tendency within the police service to see technology as a tool that helps them do the job, rather than something that can fundamentally alter the nature and context of that job, and the scope and nature of government research and development for the police have both reflected and helped to reinforce that view.[2] Diametrically opposed to this point of view is that taken by many modern commentators on policing who present policing technologies both as all-pervasive and entirely baleful, if not in intention then in their effects. For example, Sarah Manwaring-White in what is probably the most up-to-date and comprehensive source of information on policing technologies, writes in a vein which is not untypical: 'Police today rely overwhelmingly on technology and equipment.' 'The typical British bobby is now highly trained and technologically sophisticated.' 'Police no longer foster discipline within the community, they try to impose it from outside. The result is not only aggrieved or alienated sections of the community but a police force less equipped to handle aggravation and alienation, despite — indeed in part because of — its battery of technological aids.' (All quotations are from Manwaring-White, 1984, Ch. 8.) This is neither fair nor accurate and although not concerned in any detail with technology, it is one of the aims of this book to put such comments into perspective.

While my focus is a relatively narrow one, I have been concerned to set in context those aspects of policing I have examined. Thus I look in the final chapter at some features of the internal police organisation and culture which inhibit change, and earlier at two important sources of control and influence, the Home Office and Her Majesty's Inspectors of Constabulary (HMIs). Both have tended to act as a spur to innovation. Although the roles of the Home Office and HMIs are circumscribed, most notably by the constitutional independence of chief constables from political control, their power to influence policing directly is clear. The Home Secretary has a statutory duty to promote the efficiency of the police; the Home Office spends money on policing research and on common services, and it offers guidance to chief officers on matters of law, policy and practice.[3] HMIs are statutorily responsible for reporting to the Secretary of State on the efficiency of forces. It is also their job to identify 'best practice' in policing and disseminate it to the 43 forces in England and Wales.

Besides having direct powers and responsibilities, the Home Office and HMIs are also able to influence policing in numerous subtle and indirect ways. Thus while the legislative framework within which they operate has not changed, both the Home Office and the Inspectorate have, since the riots in 1981, taken a significantly more interventionist stance towards the police than had previously been the norm. I discuss this change, the various channels of influence and the carrots and sticks of persuasion and control and their relevance to innovation in Chapter 7.

Some explanation is required about what I have described as innovatory and experimental. I have defined an innovation as a planned, that is a deliberate, intended change from what has gone immediately before. In this sense, innovation may amount to simply a new means of achieving a well-established end, or it may involve something more fundamental and a great deal less common — a redefinition or reassessment of the ends or purposes for which an organisation or parts of it are said to exist. By describing a project as experimental I mean that it involves deliberate manipulations in order to achieve some predetermined aim, coupled with an attempt, however rudimentary, to assess whether that aim has been reached. Defined in this way, both innovation and experiment imply the need for research. Problems need to be defined, an existing state of affairs described and ways of reacting to it prescribed. Ideally, some way of taking stock, once the process of change is under way or completed, is also needed. One of the aims of this book is to examine how these various steps are gone through by the police in implementing programmes of change, and with what results.

In gathering material for this book I initially allowed the police to define what they saw as innovatory and experimental rather than try to impose definitions on them. This raised two difficulties. The first was that what passes as innovation in one force may be a long-standing practice in another.[4] In addition, I quickly became aware that much of what is presented and publicly debated as new is not new at all; and that virtually all the innovations described in this book have philosophical roots and practical precedents in the past. Since policing is inevitably 'conservative' and, indeed, the police service takes pride in its ability to create and sustain a traditional image of itself, this may seem no more than a statement of the obvious. There exists, however, an additional tendency to present a great deal of what passes for policing innovation as though it presents answers to policing problems which have so far eluded us. New initiatives are sold both by drawing on time-honoured justifications and assumptions about policing, and by reconstructing a past in which, in the attempt to bring about a desired future state of affairs, evidence about what was the case easily becomes distorted. This book is not intended as a history of policing. However, I have tried, as far as possible, to draw on examples from the (usually quite recent) past in order to put current innovations and experiments into perspective. This should enable readers to judge more accurately what chance these innovations stand of fulfilling the hopes which gave rise to them.

My method of study was as follows. I began with a letter to each chief officer in England and Wales describing the scope and nature of my review and asking to visit the force. I followed this up with a visit, which was usually organised by the force research and planning department (or its equivalent) and was centred around its activities. During these visits, I usually talked with someone in the force's computer project team and often met the force crime prevention officer, community liaison officer and/or the officer in charge of community involvement. On some visits I also met officers involved day to day with particular projects and schemes. Usually I spent a day with the force, although some visits lasted only half a day and some for up to a week.

As a way of describing the nature, extent and consequences of innovation my approach was inevitably far from ideal. The officers to whom I spoke during visits tended to be senior ranks in headquarters departments. I was also unable to follow through schemes that were described to me and to look independently at how they were implemented, how they affected the behaviour of individual officers and what their impact was on local communities. In so far as I was able to form a judgement on these things, I relied on documents prepared by local constabularies and by individual officers and where they were available, which was not very often, on reports by independent evaluators. Perhaps the most obvious deficiency of my method of gathering material was that it left me in a poor position to judge whether what I was told were major changes in philosophy or practice had in fact made a difference to the behaviour and attitudes of the officers who were supposed to be most affected by them. My method also ran the risk of conveying a highly police-centred view of innovation, although I have tried to minimise this risk by testing police claims against other evidence wherever possible. The method was, however, the best available given the potentially large number of projects to the documented. On the plus side, it gave me an unrivalled opportunity to talk to a large number of officers about changes in policing methods, styles and philosophies, about the need for change, the pressures to change and how the police form judgements about the effects of change.

As well as visiting forces, I tried to keep abreast of relevant developments within the Home Office and the Inspectorate of Constabulary. The Home Office coordinates and cajoles over a wide range of activity relevant to my theme and it also acts as a central point for the collection, assessment and dissemination of much of the information which I was collecting independently. I describe Home Office activities in the information field in more detail in the following chapters and list them, together with other sources of information on policing schemes, in Appendix B. Four sources of information seem worth mentioning here. The first is the Home Office Crime Prevention Centre, which has recently begun to keep an index of force crime prevention projects. The second is the Police Research Services Unit Information Desk, which keeps a computerised index of force projects and acts as a central reference point for officers wanting information on what is going on in other forces in the research and development field. Neither of these two sources is geared to producing evaluations of what they document. A third source of information on policing schemes is the Home Office Research and Planning Unit. The information it keeps is restricted to the small number of schemes that the Unit has itself researched or funded research on, but its lack of range is to some extent compensated for by the fact that the Unit is particularly strong on evaluation. A fourth source is the Home Office Crime Prevention Unit, which is establishing an information service to bring together research findings and good practice and to disseminate this information to forces.

In asking me to carry out this review, the Police Foundation assumed that, by making information about particular innovations more widely available, the review would alert forces to schemes which would otherwise remain unknown to them and thereby act as a spur to innovation. I now feel this assumption to have been misguided. Adequate sources are already available from which forces can find out what others are doing. The fact that they might not choose to implement innovative schemes is not for want of documented examples, but more to do with police attitudes (often entrenched) towards the need for and perceived purpose of change, and also the organisational impediments to implementing seemingly good ideas. There is also a second difficulty, which is the shortage of evidence available from which to judge the value of any particular scheme, a deficiency which also arises in relation to most of what is documented in this book. No police officer reading this review could justifiably conclude of most of what I have documented: 'That's a good idea. We should try that in my force, because it is likely to have such and such effect.' Prescriptions of this sort cannot be derived from the kind of evidence that has been available to me to document and review. So this cannot be a review of best, or even good practice. What I have tried to do instead is first, to understand why, given the lack of good evidence, there is nevertheless a good deal of consensus about what best practice is; and second, to examine the attitudes to the collection, analysis and assessment of evidence on which that consensus is based. An analysis of these attitudes forms a major theme of this book. Because of this, I felt it important to set out at the beginning what is known about policing and what is not known and to describe the way in which that knowledge has been obtained and what is being done with it. Hence, in the following chapter I briefly review policing research, its implications for policing practice and change and how those implications have been absorbed by the police. The chapter also looks at how the police organise their own in-house research, what topics they research, the approaches they use and what lessons they draw from the results. The next four chapters deal with specific innovations. Chapter 3 looks at the drive towards efficiency in policing, streamlining procedures, cutting out paperwork and reorganising patrols so that more officers can be returned to the beat. Chapters 4 and 5 document crime prevention initiatives. Throughout these chapters I pay attention to what is currently seen as being good practice, how those judgements are reached and what kind of information is needed to improve on them. Chapter 6 is a cautionary tale. It describes what at the time was a highly acclaimed innovation but one which has now fallen from favour — unit beat policing — and the kind of research that was done to support its introduction; and it draws some lessons from this case study both for current policing fashions and current policing research. In Chapter 7 I examine the role and interests of central government in encouraging efficient and effective policing, including how those terms are defined and made operational. Since government is interested in the rational management of resources, in the final chapter I look at the scope for applying rationality to policing and the obstacles and limits to doing so. Two forces have recently introduced a management approach to, and philosophy of, policing known as policing by objectives, which aims to maximise the rational management of resources towards clear, agreed and pre-determined ends. The chapter deals specifically with this approach both as a philosophy of policing and a practical innovation and examines some of its implications as a language for debating policing issues and as a form of accountability.

Individual projects and initiatives are listed in Appendix A. The list is confined to what might broadly be termed 'community policing' initiatives, mainly attempts to revise patrolling methods and patrolling styles in ways which are thought to be more acceptable to the public, and attempts to involve members of the public and non-police institutions in crime prevention and control. This list is not intended to be exhaustive. For a start, it includes only those initiatives which have the status of a special project, or which a force has otherwise chosen to publicise, and on which a certain minimal amount of written material is available, or likely to become available. The manner in which it was compiled (visits to police forces over a period of two years with some subsequent updating by correspondence) means that it is bound to be out of date, for some forces more than for others. The list is therefore intended to be illustrative of what is going on rather than to provide a definitive statement of it. In addition, two things happened during the course of this review which meant that the forces I visited early on (in late 1981 and throughout most of 1982) will probably have moved on from the position that I found them at; they will have initiated further projects and will have begun to think about what they do in ways which are more often and more explicitly resource-conscious. These two events are a revival of an explicit and stated interest by central government in crime prevention (see Chapter 4), which was communicated to forces in an interdepartmental circular (Home Office, 1984a) at the beginning of 1984; and, towards the end of 1982, the establishment of a new post within the police department at the Home Office to deal specifically with issues of efficiency and effectiveness in policing, subjects on which the Home Office issued a circular to police forces at the end of 1983 (Home Office, 1983c). While many forces will have begun to think about and to implement the kinds of initiatives referred to in these circulars some time in advance of their being issued, the circulars will have given fresh impetus to these initiatives as well as starting off new ways of thinking in other forces. The process of change they have started is likely to be a continuing one and I can do little more at this point than discuss its general implications, rather than document it in detail.

Notes

1. Instant cautioning schemes are a way of reducing delay by avoiding the time-consuming administrative procedures that are usually followed when decisions are made about cautioning juveniles. Schemes vary, but typically they allow decisions to be taken lower down the police hierarchy than would otherwise be the case; and they by-pass other agencies, such as social services departments, which are not consulted over the decision to caution but instead informed of it after it has been taken. Instant cautioning schemes normally apply only to certain specified categories of case. They enable juveniles to be cautioned often within hours of being apprehended, rather than after a wait of several weeks. Around half of police forces operate such schemes.

2. Perhaps for this reason, the work programme of the Home Office Scientific Research and Development Branch contains nothing on the impact of technology on the people who are policed, even though a considerable portion of the Branch's budget is devoted to helping to implement computer systems and devising and testing new and better sorts of equipment (Scientific Research and Development Branch, 1984a). The Home Office Research and Planning Unit also gives low priority to research on the social impact of policing technologies, a priority reflected not only in their 1984/85 programme of research (Home Office Research and Planning Unit, 1984, pp. 12–14) but also in statements about likely future priorities in policing research. Morris and Heal's review of research on police work and its effectiveness concludes, amongst other things, that 'there is little ground for arguing that technological innovation in policing should constitute a primary focus for future research effort.' (Morris and Heal, 1981, p. 50.)

3. The statutory duties and functions of the Secretary of State are defined by sections 28 to 43 of the Police Act 1964.

4. A good example is the use of community constables — officers who are given responsibility for working a particular beat and getting to know the people who live and work there. This form of deployment was supposed to have become established throughout the country by the late 1960s. Some forces have never abandoned it. Others have, or failed to adopt it in the first place. As a result, many forces are 'rediscovering' the community constable and are introducing (or reintroducing) new initiatives based on this deployment.

2 RESEARCH ON, FOR AND BY THE POLICE

Most institutions tend to think of their work as important and necessary and they are not given to spending too much time and effort questioning the purpose and the effectiveness of what they do. The police are no exception. They have been remarkably successful in creating an appearance of usefulness and competence, such that the value of much traditional activity — patrol, for example, and crime prevention — is hardly questioned, either by the service itself or by the public. Failures of performance are admitted but tend to be blamed on lack of manpower and of money, inadequate powers, or an intractable social or physical environment. As with all generalisations, there are exceptions to this one, but what is remarkable is the extent to which traditional policing precepts and images not only continue to set the terms of public debate but are also used to justify what are presented as new departures in policing methods and styles. As a result, many aspects of policing have remained immune from critical scrutiny and the police service has been able to discourage and rebuff the attentions of research with relative ease.

Although the police perform other functions they have customarily justified their existence and created an appearance of usefulness and competence by referring to their central place in the 'war against crime', that is, their supposed capacity to prevent offences and deter offenders. Traditionally, the police have been thought to achieve these effects through their presence, their capacity to persuade people to act in their own best interests in preventing and reporting crime, and through their role as initiators of those processes culminating in the conviction and punishment of offenders. Until quite recently, the usefulness of these activities in achieving their intended effects has been more or less taken for granted. This is now changing and a new and more sceptical consensus is emerging which casts doubt on many of the traditional assumptions about what the police do and do not do and the kinds of effects this activity has.

In this chapter I shall briefly outline what existing research has to say about police activity, and describe some of the ways in which police are being expected to take notice of and respond to this research and how its messages are being marketed, both to the police service and to a wider public. Because most of this research is underaken or funded by government and because it is being used by government to help support some of its policy initiatives, I have chosen to concentrate more on government research than on research undertaken in universities and polytechnics and in independent research institutes. This is not to say that independent research is of no importance; it is simply a recognition of the fact that academic police researchers have been left to plough a lonely furrow. Those interested in doing research on the police have found it difficult to gain access or a receptive audience for what they have to say amongst those who often stand to benefit most from it: the police themselves. I refer below to some of the reasons for this state of affairs. Finally, I discuss the kinds of research the police do for themselves, why they do it, why it needs to change and what some of the pressures for change are.

Government research for the police and on the police

Most research on policing in England and Wales is undertaken by the Home Office through its Scientific Research and Development Branch (SRDB) and its Research and Planning Unit (RPU). Of the two, the SRDB spends the more money, has a longer tradition of research activity, and has a closer relationship with the police service.

Scientific Research and Development Branch

The origins of SRDB lie in the 1962 *Final Report* of the Royal Commission on the Police which commented that

> the amount of money at present devoted to research into police problems is insignificant compared with the cost of the research programmes of the fighting services, and the community should . . . accept the burden of a properly conducted programme of research (para. 241).

The Commission recommended the establishment of a central government unit, working under the Chief Inspector of Constabulary, which would help plan police methods, develop new equipment and study new techniques. The unit would help to create a climate conducive to innovation by ensuring that 'the results of research are not only made available but speedily adopted throughout the country'. The Commission envisaged 'a constant two-way flow of ideas between the unit and chief constables, so that fresh information can be made quickly available throughout the police service' (para. 242).

The Home Office Police Research and Planning Branch (the precursor of SRDB) was set up in 1963 as a result of the Commission's recommendations.[1] It was charged with thinking about how the police service could make the most productive use of its manpower and what to do about the 'grave problem of serious and unsolved crime' (Critchley, 1978, p. 292). Most of its staff were police officers (there were five of them plus two civilian scientists) and it concentrated its research efforts on central operational issues such as CID methods and the effectiveness of foot patrol. Its work on the latter was later to contribute to the design and implementation of unit beat policing, an innovation in which the Branch played a large part (see Chapter 6).

Since it was set up the Branch has been expanded and reorganised with a view to making its research more operationally relevant and to improving its liaison with forces. The emphasis of its work has changed, becoming increasingly (not to say abstrusely) technical. Within a few years of being established, the Branch had taken on the responsibility which had previously rested with the Association of Chief of Police Officers for designing and testing new items of policing equipment. It expanded its laboratory facilities and increased its scientific staff. By the early 1970s, technical research and development, including computer development, had come to dominate the Branch's work and has continued to do so ever since. In 1984, the Branch employed between 80 and 90 technical and scientific staff on policing research. Of its budget of £5 million, about one-quarter went on computer development and most of the remainder on other technical research. Less than one-tenth was devoted to broader and non-technical questions of operational effectiveness. In recent years such research has included studies of police management roles, of the kinds of information available to police management and how it is and is not used, and of the effects of redeploying officers on foot patrol.[2]

The Branch has always placed greater priority on developing and nurturing relationships with the police service than on creating for itself any significant public profile or on contributing directly to the quality of public debate on the police. Its reports are not formally published (though they are usually available on request) and their existence is not widely known outside the police service. The Branch's research agenda is negotiated and agreed directly with the police service, formally through the Technical Services and the Computer Development Committees of the Association of Chief Police Officers, and informally through a process of consultation with individual forces. The Branch has attached much importance not only to doing research of practical value to the police but also to disseminating the results of its work to them. While one result of these priorities is a research agenda which is relatively unthreatening to police assumptions about themselves, it has also allowed the Branch to act as a potentially influential means of conveying research messages to forces and to help create in them a more empirically-minded culture. Thus, around a dozen middle and senior ranking police officers are currently seconded from their forces to work with the Branch. In the early days, these officers worked closely with the Branch's civilian scientists under the direction of a senior police officer. Today they are organisationally distinct as the Police Research Services Unit (PRSU), but their functions remain essentially the same: to liaise between the SRDB scientists and the police service; to find out what research the police service wants and what it thinks of the research already being undertaken by the Branch; to do research themselves; and to keep the police up to date with all relevant research (see Openshaw, 1981). One of PRSU's most important functions is to maintain an information desk which keeps a centralised record of what policing research is going on and who is doing it, and acts as a clearing house and contact agency for individual police forces wanting to undertake research themselves. It is hoped by this means to encourage better research and to create a greater awareness by forces of one another's experiments and innovations. A quarterly *Information Desk Bulletin* is circulated to forces and is used to disseminate and trawl for relevant material (see Ryan 1980/81; and Ryan and Wheatley 1980/81).

Home Office Research and Planning Unit

The philosophy and remit of SRDB stand in contrast to the tradition of policing research developed elsewhere in the Home Office, in its Research and Planning Unit. The RPU spends comparatively little on policing research: its annual expenditure on it is less than 10 per cent of SRBD's.[3] The Unit also spends its money on very different kinds of research. It has concentrated on questions of operational effectiveness, particularly in the area of crime prevention, and, increasingly, on finding out what it is that the police do and how their consumers react to it. Unlike SRDB, the RPU has worked in relative isolation from the police. Until very recently, it has never seen them as direct clients for its work, nor even necessarily as an important audience for it. The Research Unit's research programme is negotiated with very little direct police input within the Home Office, ostensibly in accordance with the customer-contractor principle set out in the Rothschild report on government research and development (HMSO, 1971).[4] In practice, the Unit has had much more leeway in defining and creating its own work programme than a strict application of this principle allows. It has traditionally fought for independence from what it has tended to see as the rather narrow administrative concerns of the Home Office police department in order to try and produce a body of work which is intellectually coherent and politically persuasive in its own terms. It has had considerable success with this strategy. The result is a more iconclastic research tradition than SRDB's and a correspondingly greater concern with publishing the results of its work and in reaching the widest possible audience. In comparison with SRDB, the RPU has not sought out the police as a privileged or special audience, nor has it given priority to developing channels of communication with them. For its part, the police service has shown little interest in learning about the Unit's work.[5]

The Unit has paid for its relative aloofness with problems in gaining access to police forces. It is only since 1979, beginning with the work it did on police interrogation for the Royal Commission on Criminal Procedure (Softley *et al.*, 1980) that the Unit has become involved in work where its researchers have much face-to-face contact with police officers. Difficulties of access have forced the Unit to concentrate its efforts on crime prevention, which is a relatively low-profile and uncontroversial area of policing, and on research based on secondary sources, mainly statistical analyses and literature reviews. However, this view from the sidelines has enabled the Unit to produce a body of work which is a great deal more critical of traditional assumptions than might otherwise have been the case; and also to act as an official channel for expressing some of the more troubling research messages which have originated from the research world outside the Home Office. In these respects, three of the Unit's publications are crucial. They are *Designing out crime* (Clarke and Mayhew, 1980), *Crime control and the police* (Morris and Heal, 1981) and *Crime and police effectiveness* (Clarke and Hough, 1984).

This work is important for two main reasons. First, the picture of police work which emerges from it differs quite a lot from the public's ideas of it and police characterisations of it. And second, it succcessfully questions many of the assumptions that are commonly made about the ability of the police to deter criminals and prevent crime.

One of the main casualties of the Unit's work and other independent studies is the idea that the police are engaged in a war against crime in which their main weapons are their capacity to enforce the law and their commitment to doing so. In practice, law-enforcement and crime-related work form a relatively small proportion of police patrol work, which is directed instead to responding to calls from members of the public. Most of these calls are not to do with crime, but are requests for help and advice on a wide variety of incidents which, for various reasons, people feel unable to deal with. Many commentators have used these kinds of findings to characterise policing more as social service work than law-enforcement work and to suggest that the public image of the police (and ultimately their effectiveness) depend crucially — even primarily — on how well they carry out their duty to advise, assist and befriend. For their part, senior police officers have chosen increasingly to stress the importance of service images of policing in public representations of themselves, and to stress the police role as benevolent and a helping one.

But whatever the realities of practical police work, the primary object of the police force remains to prevent crime. Traditionally the police have been thought to achieve this through the deterrent effect of their presence on patrol and through their capacity to persuade other people to act in their own best interests by taking simple crime preventive precautions. Neither strategy works as well as is often assumed.

First, patrol. Here it seems that the number of officers patrolling an area makes very little difference to the amount of crime that takes place there. Some gains can be achieved by 'saturation patrolling', that is, by flooding an area with officers, but such patrols are costly to maintain for long and any effects they have on crime tend to be short-lived ones. There is also little evidence favouring the effectiveness of foot patrol over car patrol (or vice versa) either in deterring crime or reducing it. The reasons for this lie in the nature both of crime and of people's perceptions of policing. Aggregate crime figures may look large but, in relation to time and place, criminal acts are relatively rare events. Their rarity means that they are not readily susceptible of being discovered by routine patrols which, because of the amount of ground they have to cover, are bound to be sparse and intermittent. The likelihood of a patrolling officer coming across a crime in progress is slight. The impact that officers have on people's perceptions of a police presence are also not very high. For most people, everyday patrol activity appears to be a pretty low-profile affair: they neither know nor notice a great deal about how their area is policed. This low visibility of patrol clearly reduces its deterrent potential.

If the police cannot easily deter by their presence, can they nevertheless prevent crimes occurring? In the crime prevention field, the police have set great store on exhorting people to be more security conscious and on providing advice on physical security to institutions and to ordinary householders. Some of this effort has been successful but a great deal has not. The problem is simply that people's awareness of the risks of falling victim to crime is often not high enough to prompt them to take action which will minimise those risks. It seems to be difficult to change this state of affairs. Crime prevention propaganda can change people's attitudes to security, but more security-conscious behaviour by no means follows. In short, people seem remarkably resistant to acting in what crime prevention planners perceive to be their own best interests. Good security has costs — in money, time and convenience — which discourage people from attaching high priority to it.

Translating research into policy

The incorporation of research findings into a new body of accepted wisdom is a slow and uneven process in which the intellectual persuasiveness of the research is a great deal less relevant than its political appeal. So far as the police service goes, research findings are unlikely to make an impact unless and until the police feel they have something to gain from taking notice of them. In the past, the police have tended to be suspicious of research and have looked to research neither to provide useful information about themselves, nor to inform their own policy initiatives.[6] Policing culture is an essentially pragmatic one, valuing action over reflection. Like anyone else, the police have been more receptive to information that helps to justify their activity rather than that which turns a critical eye on it. The less-than-flattering picture of policing activity that much independent research has given has probably served to strengthen attitudes of suspicion towards outsiders and has done little to counteract a widespread belief within the police service that only police officers may legitimately comment on policing matters. Research has not, on the whole, told the police what they wanted to hear. It is not just the message which has been unpalatable. It is also that research deals in a language which is very different from that used in everyday policing; and it operates at a level of generality which is simply unconvincing to those whose experience derives from having to deal with the immediate and the particular. Thus many police officers with managerial responsibilities continue to see the seat of the pants as a greater repository of practical wisdom than inferences drawn from empirical research. Much of this is now changing. Part of this change is due to increased professionalism, part to a recognition that defensiveness can compound misunderstanding while greater openness can counteract it, and part to the requirement that the police now account in the language of objectives and demonstrable achievements. So how, broadly, can research help the police? There are a number of ways. First, by drawing attention to the importance of their service role it can help the police present a more caring image of themselves. An emphasis on service of course raises questions about how police performance might be judged using criteria other than the traditional ones of arrests and detections. Research can help in the development of these criteria. It should also help the police better to explain why it is that they are unable in many circumstances to deal effectively with crime. This in turn will provide (and has already provided) them with a platform from which to enlist the help of others in reaching their objectives. Finally, the application of research methods should help the police to plan and judge the effects of their own activity better.

Are the police taking advantage of the sorts of help research can give them? In practice, while they are coming round to research, the sort of studies they undertake, typically through force research and planning departments, are very limited.

Police research and planning

One striking feature of most of the research which I have summarised so far is how little of it has been initiated or carried out by the police themselves. Yet all forces have a department onto which some kind of planning, co-ordinating and research responsibilities devolve. These departments provide virtually the only resource within the police service for systematically monitoring and evaluating its own activities and performance. Their size and remit and the kind of work they do are, therefore, important indicators of how seriously the police take these functions.

The typical force planning department is small — a team of perhaps four police officers and a civilian clerk, with a superintendent at its head. Some teams are much larger than this, especially in the larger forces, but others are smaller. Since research and statistical skills tend to be more common outside than inside the police service, it might be expected that many research and planning posts would be held by civilians. However, although some departments employ civilian staff, this is not the norm and, where civilians exist, they are very much in the minority.[7] Research and planning in the police service is overwhelmingly dominated by police officers. This balance is favoured by the police themselves who argue that they are more in touch with the practicalities of police work than are civilians and that too high a proportion of civilians would undermine their department's credibility with the rest of the force.

Although most research and planning departments are small, this is of lesser consequence than their remit. Many are concerned more with administration than with research, some exclusively so. Thus a typical research and planning department will be responsible for designing new forms, issuing new force orders and revamping old ones, running the force suggestion scheme and overseeing the force building programme. Where a large capital project is under way, such as the procurement, design and building of a new force headquarters, this may account for all the team's work. In addition, numerous small jobs which have no other obvious organisational home tend to gravitate to research and planning departments. Many departmental heads would be unlikely to cavil at the description of their empires as dustbin departments. This state of affairs is not only a reflection of how seriously many forces take research and planning functions, it also limits these departments' capacity to do more relevant work.

Aside from administration, much of the work undertaken by research and planning departments is aimed at improving organisational efficiency. This may involve streamlining procedures and administration, reviewing geographical boundaries between divisions and beats, or reassigning manpower within and between departments, operational units and ranks. This bias is reflected in the kinds of requests for research information that departments make of the PRSU Information Desk. The great majority are for information about technical equipment, routine procedures and administrative matters. Such activities can of course be of considerable organisational importance. In some forces, for example where an incoming chief constable wants to put his own stamp on force organisation, research and planning departments will be charged with undertaking major efficiency reviews and will be used as the cutting edge of organisational change. This latter aspect of their work forms a major and explicit part of some departments' remit.[8]

Although there are exceptions, research and planning departments have not on the whole been greatly concerned with thinking about or measuring organisational effectiveness. Instead their research is almost exclusively concerned with improving internal management and making it more businesslike rather than with improving police performance. As the initiatives described in Chapter 3 show, it is usually taken for granted that greater effectiveness will follow once procedures have been improved and more efficient ways of doing things implemented. In so far as they *are* required to monitor and evaluate new initiatives within forces, many police officers are apt to engage in what might be termed 'foregone conclusion' research, that is the seeking out of research information to support a preferred course of action rather than analysing the necessity for it and the results of it. As I hope to demonstrate, the reputations of several well-known policing initiatives rest less on any carefully considered evaluation of their effectiveness than on a fudging of ambiguous or inadequate data and on good publicity. There are often good reasons for this. Any department whose job is to uncover and rectify deficiencies in the way things are being done has a potentially difficult relationship with the rest of the force. This can seriously blunt its critical edge. Nor is the situation helped by the lack of research expertise within forces, although this difficulty is now being recognised and faced up to. Thus forces are being urged to seek outside help when planning and researching their own initiatives and are being invited to consider a wider range of research methodologies in researching them.[9] Such developments will help to improve methodological rigour and broaden forces' research base. In addition, a number of recent Home Office initiatives (to be discussed in later chapters) have implications for the kind of research that is done on the police and the kind of research the police do for themselves. Taken overall, the effects of these initiatives should be to raise the status and importance of policing research, to create a demand for research information by police themselves, and to encourage the police to use research-based arguments in place of traditional assertion.

So far as policing research goes, these initiatives mark a distinct shift from what has gone before. Yet it would be foolish to ignore the obstacles to establishing a greater research consciousness in forces. The capacity to take stock is built into very few policing activities and operations; while the desire to do so sits uneasily with the police's need to create a picture of their own successes and a sense of pride in their own achievements. For these reasons, and because of the lack of research expertise within forces, it seems likely that the main impetus for critical research and much of the capability for carrying it out will continue to come from outside the police service. It seems less likely, however, that this research will continue to happen by stealth, as has so often been the case in the past. Instead, what seems increasingly likely is a slowly developing rapprochement between police officers interested in what research can tell them about their own activity, and their erstwhile civilian critics.

Notes

1. The statutory authority is section 42 of the Police Act 1964, which enables the Home Secretary to 'set up such bodies and take such other steps as appear to be necessary or expedient for the purpose of undertaking research into matters affecting the efficiency of the police'.

2. Details of its work are published in the Branch's annual research programme. Information on the Branch's expenditure is derived from Table 1 in *Police Research Programme 1984/85*, Scientific Research and Development Branch, 1984a. This table summarises the cost of internal research in man-years and external research in terms of expenditure. I have used the Treasury ready reckoner figure of £25,000 per employee to arrive at a figure for expenditure on internal research.

3. The RPU does not publish such a detailed breakdown of its expenditure and staffing as does SRDB so that it is difficult to make a precise comparison. In 1984/85 the Unit's budget for all criminal justice research was approximately £1.5 million split almost evenly between internal and external projects. It seems reasonable to assume that not more than one-quarter of this sum was committed to research directly on or related to policing. See Home Office Research and Planning Unit *Research Programme* 1984–85, p. 12ff.

4. The customer-contractor principle requires the customer for research to say what he wants and the contractor to do it. In the RPU's case, the customer is usually the Home Office police department.

5. A pointed example is provided by the fate of *The police response to calls from the public* (Ekblom and Heal), published in 1982. This study documents how police radio controllers, the first point of contact for members of the public who telephone the police for help, deal with people's requests. It also set out to assess whether calls could readily be 'graded', so as to distinguish those where a quick response was necessary from those where less urgent response, if any, would do. Since many forces claim to have implemented or to be in the process of implementing systems of graded response and all forces are under pressure to think about how best they might manage their resources, this report might well be considered to be required reading for many officers. The initial circulation of the report was around 50 copies, one for each chief officer and one for each of half-a-dozen or so other officers known to be interested in it. In the eighteen months or so following publication a total of 15 additional copies were circulated, at their request, to seven police forces. (The report is free.) This resounding lack of interest was undermined only by one force, which ordered 250 copies of the report to be circulated to every officer of, and above, the rank of chief superintendent. (Since these figures were compiled, at least one other force is known to have given the report an equally wide circulation.)

6. See, for example, strictures made by Sir Cyril Philips in his 1979 James Smart lecture. Referring to the quality of police submissions to the Royal Commission on Criminal Procedure, he said: 'a very great proportion . . . is based either and most often on simple assertion, and sometimes on arguments from principle unsupported by specific, verifiable evidence or on anecdotes, not on research conducted into the pre-trial system as it actually works. Nowhere is the day-to-day experience on which police views rest presented in a form which shows that an attempt has been made objectively to observe and analyse them.'

7. Except in the Metropolitan Police, whose management services department is staffed virtually entirely by civilians — it also has a civilian head.

8. See for example, the Hampshire Constabulary force review team. Announcing its formation, the chief constable wrote:

> In an effort to improve on the already high quality of service we provide, I have established a Force Review Team, whose members have been personally directed by me to examine in detail our policy and procedures. Hopefully, the team, helped by all members of the Force will be able to make recommendations which will maximise the

effectiveness of our limited resources.

The team's early work addressed the following questions:

Is it possible to make more appropriate and effective use of our manpower and equipment?
Can paperwork be simplified and reduced?
Is there a need for more flexible methods of policing?
Are we, as an organisation, over-specialised?
By identifying patterns of crime and incidents can better deployments be made both to prevent and detect crime?
Should more emphasis be given to preventive aspects of police work?

9. See for example Males, 1982a. A recent Home Office circular specifically invites chief officers to consider seeking advice from outside the force in researching policing initiatives (Home Office, 1983c). In addition, a circular letter from Her Majesty's Chief Inspector of Constabulary recommends public surveys as a means of obtaining information on unreported crime and on public attitudes to police. Since 1982, the Police Staff College has regularly run two-week-long methods courses for research and planning officers. Another recent innovation is the College's rolling programme which is aimed at teaching officers to do research as part of a programme of instigating and managing change within their own forces. Officers spend a fortnight at the college being introduced to the ways and means of analysing problems before returning to their forces to plan a project. They are then recalled to the college at regular intervals to discuss progress.

3 ON THE BEAT

Patrol is the backbone of police work. Every police officer starts on the beat and patrol absorbs a larger proportion of manpower than any other policing function.[1] For most people the visibility and behaviour of patrol officers provide the most concrete evidence available to them that policing is being done. The way patrol officers behave is seen as being crucial to the state of police public relations. The behaviour and comportment of patrol officers also serve an important symbolic purpose: the beat officer is used to evoke a set of images which provide a potent source of legitimation of the police function. For all these reasons, changing and experimenting with how patrol is organised have tended to be recurrent preoccupations of those charged with managing police resources or otherwise thinking about what the police should do. Patrol thus provides a relatively fruitful source of policing innovations and illustrates a wide range of issues to do with the nature of policing tasks and how these can be more efficiently and effectively organised.

Each force organises its patrol strength rather differently and there are also differences within forces according to the nature and type of area policed. However, certain basic principles apply. Round-the-clock cover is provided by officers who work shifts and who patrol either on foot or in cars. Their job is to respond to calls from members of the public and to maintain a visible street presence. Area beat officers, who also normally patrol on foot, are given responsibility for policing a particular area and (within limits) choose their own hours of work. Unlike shift-based officers whose work is alternately passive (to all intents and purposes, doing nothing) and reactive (responding to calls), area beat officers are expected to get to know the people who live and work on their beat. They may also carry out more general patrol duties and some criminal investigation work.

I shall examine three main types of patrol innovation in this chapter. The first concerns those activities aimed at increasing patrol strength. Most chief officers openly espouse the virtues of returning more officers to the beat. I shall look at how and why they are doing so and with what apparent effects. A second, related change involves attempts to alter the balance between different types of patrol — mostly away from car patrol and in favour of general foot or area beat patrols. A third type of innovation is aimed at altering the type and purpose of activities undertaken

22

by patrols and making them more useful, effective and purposeful. None of these types of change is as distinct as is implied above and most of the initiatives described below involve elements of all three. Thus, for example, a policy of returning more officers to the beat almost always rests on judgements that they will do more valuable work there. A major theme of this chapter is how the police arrive at these judgements, whether they are justified and how they might be improved.

The onward march of foot patrol

A difficulty that stands in the way of assessing virtually all recent patrol innovations is that they assume what they ought to set out to prove, namely that having officers out and about patrolling on foot is the best use of police resources. This assumption is so widely held that to question it seems perverse. Yet the history (and certainly the recent history) of patrol can be seen as one of reaction to the perceived disadvantages of foot patrol. In 1971, the Home Secretary responded with an unequivocal 'No' to a parliamentary question asking whether 'in view of the recent increase in pay awarded to the constabulary, he will recommend to all Chief Constables that as many policemen as possible should cover their beats on foot instead of by use of panda cars'.[2] The Home Office view then was that foot patrol was outmoded, that it failed to provide flexible cover and was an uneconomic and inefficient use of manpower.

In Chapter 6 I shall look in some detail at why in the 1960s foot patrol fell from official favour. The case against it was essentially an economic one. It should come as no surprise therefore that foot patrol is being rehabilitated at a time when economic factors favour it. When the large increases in oil prices in the mid-1970s made vehicle patrols more expensive, many chief officers began to look at foot patrol to solve some of their financial problems. Forces were under pressure to cut back on expenditure and they looked to vehicle mileage restrictions and cutting vehicle fleets to save money. Furthermore, by the end of the 1970s and in the early 1980s many forces were enjoying a recruitment boom as a result of the substantial increases in police pay recommended by the Edmund Davies Committee and accepted by the government.[3] In the four years 1978–82, overall police strength rose from 107,847 to 119,531, an increase of 10 per cent. Once they have completed their training, newly recruited officers are assigned to foot patrol: it is where they learn the job. Thus any upsurge in recruiting is translated directly — at least in the short term — into an increase in the number of officers patrolling on foot.

Provided the manpower is available, foot patrol therefore makes economic sense. But it also has other attractions. The return of more officers to foot patrol has coincided with a period when it seems hard to find anyone with a good word to say for vehicle patrols. Putting police officers into cars is widely regarded as having created an unprecedented gulf between police and public and to have limited, or even removed, opportunity for day to day interaction. It is felt, too, to have created a police response to problems which stresses reaction and containment at the expense not only of good community relations but also of the police officer's primary task — that of preventing crime.[4] The words used to characterise vehicle patrol — response, reaction and fire-brigade policing — invariably carry negative connotations. Deploying, or redeploying officers on foot is therefore held to be a good way of improving the police image and of reversing the unfortunate effects of fire-brigading. It is expected to change the context in which police-public interactions occur, and to create the time and opportunity for more preventive work — following up problems, giving greater continuity of service and seeing policing problems in the round, not just as one-off incidents. These arguments are of course most fully developed in relation to the work of area beat officers. Such officers can most readily be seen to epitomise what, in Alderson's phrase, constitutes the proper 'demeanour for policing'. They draw their authority not from the safety in numbers provided by fire-brigade tactics but instead from their physical and moral qualities: self-reliance, self-control, judgement, sensitivity, fairness, courage and overall caring instinct (Alderson, 1979, Ch. 3). In embodying and practising these virtues they give expression to and reinforce society's commitment to a policing ideal.

These characterisations of the relative merits of car and foot patrol underlie a good deal of public debate and are rarely examined critically. They inform, implicitly or explicitly, much of the research that forces have carried out (or been party to) on their own patrol initiatives. Because they form part of a set of assumptions from which many commentators proceed, they make the effectiveness of force patrol initiatives peculiarly difficult to assess. I shall draw attention to this problem in describing particular initiatives.

Five patrol initiatives

I have argued above that the greater availability of officers to undertake patrol is a consequence of changes in the patterns of recruitment. However, many forces have also sought to increase patrol manpower generally and foot patrol manpower in particular, by reorganising and rationalising internal procedures and methods of work. A certain amount of experimentation has gone on in redrawing beat boundaries, revising shift cover, cutting down and delegating paperwork and reducing the number of vehicles which are available for patrol. These kinds of initiatives can expect to gain wider currency as forces come under increasing pressure to demonstrate that they are efficiently organised. Whether the end result is greater 'value for money' (as is usually implied) depends on answers to a whole set of other questions which the police service has hardly begun to formulate. For the most part, efficiency initiatives have been pursued as if they raised no significant questions about how the time and resources thus released could be most effectively used. Not surprisingly, given the nature of police research and planning, forces have been more concerned to pursue the question: how can more patrol be done? than in asking the more fundamental and more difficult ones: how can we know whether patrol activity is useful? and how do we know whether it is being done well?

My choice of five force patrol initiatives reflects the kinds of questions forces have pursued. Thus I first describe exercises in three forces (West Midlands Police, West Mercia Police and Hampshire Constabulary) which were undertaken with the intention of increasing efficiency by making more police officers available at the times of day when there is more demand for police services and/or by reducing the amount of paperwork which officers had to do. These initiatives can be taken as representative of many forces' thinking and practice but they are perhaps better documented and more self-analytical than most. In describing them I have tried to indicate what questions they leave unanswered and to suggest what further information might fill the gaps.

The fourth and fifth initiatives (in Lancashire Constabulary and the West Midlands Police) are rather different. In both of these initiatives, questions of patrol effectiveness were uppermost in the minds of those who undertook to evaluate them, although in each case the questions were answered using very different techniques. I shall discuss the evaluation of the Skelmersdale (Lancashire) policing project at some length because it epitomises an approach to evaluating policing initiatives which is not uncommon, and because it makes assumptions about the nature of police work which it ought to be the job of research to test more adequately. The Chelmsley Wood (West Midlands) initiative is important because the research on it was devised as a model for those intending to undertake evaluations of new policing schemes. It also illustrates a more general point which is applicable to most of what is described in this book. This is that the incidence of policing successes tends to be in inverse proportion to the rigour with which policing schemes are evaluated. I conclude the chapter with a set of questions about the nature and point of patrol which are raised by the five initiatives.

The West Midlands Police resource experiments

The scheme

In 1981, the West Midlands Police ran a series of experiments in which the balance of patrol cover between car and foot and at different times of the day was experimentally varied (West Midlands Police, 1982; Bond, 1982). Each of the experiments was different and involved anything from minor changes in when officers were allowed to take rest days, to more substantial alterations in permanent beat officer establishment and the number of patrol vehicles available to respond to calls. Most of the experiments ran for six months and twelve sub-divisions took part.

Two main assumptions underlay the experiments. First it was felt that the traditional shift system provided little flexibility in allocating manpower, that demand for police service had peaks and troughs which followed regular and predictable patterns and that more flexible ways should be tried of matching the availability of officers to the demands of the work. A second assumption was that foot patrol was a better form of deployment than patrolling by car because of its supposed superior preventive effects and because the public preferred it. It seems safe to assume as well that those who devised the experiments thought that vehicles were a wasteful method of responding to calls which could be dealt with equally well by officers on foot.

Reallocating manpower

In three experiments normal shift cover was reduced on Sundays, traditionally a quiet time which officers were expected to take as a rest day. In another experiment, overlapping shifts were introduced, maximising cover at busy times of the day, especially in the early evening. In a further seven experiments, the appointment of additional permanent beat officers (who were expected to schedule their shifts so as to fall between the hours of 8 a.m. and 2 a.m.) ensured relatively greater policing cover during the day, evenings and at night than in the early hours of the morning.

Increasing foot-cover

In seven sub-divisions the manning of permanent beat officer beats was increased so that many beats were double-manned or treble-manned. Overall, the number of permanent beat officers was increased from 99 to 173. Eighteen patrol and response vehicles were withdrawn from use and a proportion of those remaining were subject to mileage restrictions.

The evaluation

To evaluate the effects of the experiments, the West Midlands Police used two main sources of data. The first consisted of readily available or specially collected statistics on the distribution of work between various types of patrol, on how long it took to respond to incidents, on recorded crime, process and arrests and on assaults and complaints against the police. In addition, several hundred constables and their supervisors were asked for their views about the point and usefulness of the scheme they had taken part in; and they were also asked to assess what kinds of effects the experiments had had on the standards and effectiveness of policing. No attempts were made to assess public reactions to the schemes.

The results show a rather jaundiced acceptance by operational officers of the merits of experimenting with more flexible systems of policing, and considerable scepticism about the schemes' likely effects.[5] A majority of officers recognised the desirability in principle of trying and testing different forms of deployment, but were less than enthusiastic about participating themselves: most would have preferred not to have taken part in the experiments had they been given the choice. The system of overlapping shifts was especially unpopular. Most officers predicted it would be a 'total failure', one of the shifts had to be abandoned because of its unpopularity and officers who worked the overlapping shifts proved difficult to supervise. Questioned when the experiments were over, less than one-third of the officers who had taken part in them felt that the changes had been beneficial. Most felt that the new deployments had increased the amount of work they had to do, and about half felt that they had resulted in the public receiving less help than before and a less effective service overall. Only a few officers believed that the experiments resulted in the public getting an improved service and more readily available help.

Obviously, comments such as these may mark little more than officers' personal dissatisfaction with changes in their working patterns and a distrust of so-called improvements designed by others but which they were expected to implement. However, the statistics also gave indications (for what they are worth) that all was not necessarily well. In particular, recorded crime increased in all the experimental areas over the course of the experiment: the increases varied between 3 per cent and 36 per cent. Despite these increases, fewer suspects were apprehended or served with a summons and in one sub-division, where officers were required to patrol more on foot, the drop in the number of summonses issued amounted to almost one-half. Without further information (for example, on trends in non-experimental sub-divisions and data which do not depend solely on recorded crime), it seems idle to speculate on the reasons for these changes, although, on the face of it, they do little to support the supposed superiority of foot over car patrols.

On the plus side, the experiments — particularly those involving increased permanent beat officer cover and reduced vehicle cover — were successful in two ways. First, they saved money. The estimated savings in the capital cost of cars withdrawn from the service was £70,000 and there would also have been savings in fuel and in vehicle maintenance. Second, the experiments succeeded in increasing the amount of response policing carried out by foot patrols and hence reduced the proportion carried out by car patrols. Foot beat officers responded to 61 per cent more calls during the experiment than in an equivalent six months before it. This shift in response patterns was achieved with only a slight increase in the amount of time it took officers to respond to calls. This change occurred in all experimental areas.

Wider implications of the resource experiments

It is difficult to draw out the wider implications of these resource experiments. In a number of them, more than one experimental manipulation was applied, making it difficult to disentangle possible effects. Those effects are in any case difficult to discern given the large amount of data which was collected and the lack of any explicitly stated hypotheses which might help in interpretation. Little thought seems to have been given either to the kinds of effects that might have resulted from the experimental manipulations, or to what data should have been collected to test for these effects. As a result it is hard to see what basis there might be for either continuing or discontinuing the experiments, or for extending them force-wide.

The West Mercia Police operational support unit

In 1982, West Mercia Police began a six-month experiment in one sub-division aimed at freeing operational officers of administrative and clerical work (West Mercia Police, 1983). At the time of experiments, the operational strength of the sub-division was about 150 officers, of whom four-fifths were PCs. The new operational support unit comprised 15 staff, 12 of whom were civilians. The functions of the unit were to decide, on the basis of reports submitted by patrol constables through their supervising sergeants, what action to take in the case of traffic accidents, and minor incidents such as common assault and sudden deaths; to follow up any additional inquiries needed in relation to such cases (such as interviewing accused drivers); to liaise with the courts; and to keep relevant records.

The experiment aimed to:

increase man-hour availability for outside patrol;
increase supervisors' (sergeants and inspectors) availability for supervision and training;
ensure standardisation and consistency in decision making; and
increase efficiency in following up certain sorts of inquiries and in completing files,

and it was evaluated in two ways. Officers taking part were asked for their views of it, including whether they noticed any changes in how they spent their time. Time spent on patrol and on other duties was also measured independently and some simple workload measures were taken.

In terms of its main aim — to increase officers' availability for patrol work — the operational support unit was an undoubted success. Virtually all the constables who were asked about the scheme felt that they were spending less time clerking and more time patrolling. This impression was supported by the statistics, which showed that the percentage of time that officers spent on patrol had risen from 57 to 77, an equivalent in patrol strength of 23 additional officers. This gain was achieved almost entirely at the expense of time spent on paperwork connected with traffic accidents and minor process. Officers had originally spent 21 per cent of their time on this and with the establishment of the new unit the proportion fell to 3 per cent (West Mercia Police, 1983, Appendix E).

The reasons for these changes are not fully discussed in the report and this strongly implies that the new administrative system was thought to be entirely responsible for them. However, other changes occurred which could independently have affected the amount of time officers spent doing paperwork and hence the apparent effectiveness of the operational support unit in reducing it. These changes were a fall in the number of prosecutions on the sub-division (those in connection with traffic accidents fell by 27 per cent and for minor process offences by 22 per cent); and a marked drop in not guilty pleas (from 24 per cent to 4 per cent in respect of traffic cases and from 12 per cent to 7 per cent in respect of minor process offences). It is not clear whether this apparent change in pro-secution practice resulted from deliberate changes in policy instigated by the operational support unit, was an unintended consequence of changes in administrative procedures, or resulted from changes in the reporting practice of patrolling constables or from any other factor. In the absence of such information, it is therefore difficult to draw hard and fast conclusions about the efficacy of civilianising police posts in reducing the amount of paperwork done by police officers.

The Havant policing scheme

Like the two schemes described above, the Havant scheme started from the assumption that putting more officers back on patrol was a good thing. It also aimed to define and maximise the benefits of having them there: 'A more professional and exacting approach [than hitherto] is vital to the future of the police service.' 'Our . . . priority must be to assist . . . officers to make the best use of their patrol time and thereby increase both their satisfaction in their job and their status within the service' (Hampshire Constabulary 1981, para. 7.1).

The scheme had five main aims:

to return more officers to foot and cycle patrol;
to achieve closer contacts with the community;
to increase and improve sergeants' supervision of constables;
to increase cooperation between the uniform and specialist (particularly CID and traffic) branches;
to develop a 'better disciplined' response to calls for service from the public (ibid., paras. 2.1 to 2.5).

These aims were to be achieved in three ways: by reorganising shift cover, reducing mobile response and cutting down on patrol sergeants' paperwork, thus enabling them to spend more time out on patrol.

The scheme began with an analysis of the distribution throughout the day of calls for police assistance and the way in which the police respond-ed to those calls. It was found that only a minority (10 to 15 per cent) of calls for help were made between midnight and 8 a.m., yet as many (sometimes more) officers were on duty during these hours as at busier times. Nor did beat areas necessarily correspond to the pattern of demand, some quiet areas being relatively over-policed and busy ones under-policed. So far as police response went, over 90 per cent of calls were answered by officers in a car. It was felt that this kind of blanket response 'apparently regardless of the triviality of the call or the actual need for a vehicle' was not only unnecessarily costly, it could also damage police-public relations (ibid., para. 3.5). In addition to this pattern of response, area beat officers, the only officers with a day-to-day commitment to and responsibility for particular beats, were more often than not unavailable to work their beats. In a survey of ten area beats over a one-month period, it was found that on eight out of ten days there was no beat cover at all because officers were on leave, or on courses, or had been required to perform other duties.

In addition to the analysis of deployment statistics, operational officers were canvassed for their views on the proposed scheme. The general conclusions of this survey were that officers wanted greater stress on traditional 'bobbying' through contact with the public, less patrolling by car and more patrolling by sergeants and by officers attached to and responsible for particular beats.

The scheme

The foundations of the Havant scheme were its area beat officers, who patrolled on pedal and motor cycles. Under the scheme, the number of area beat officers doubled and supervisors were discouraged from using them as a pool of spare manpower: they were expected to spend most of their time on the beat rather than filling in for absent colleagues. Twenty-four hour response cover was maintained by a reduced number of vehicle patrols and, in town centres, by foot patrols. The despatching of cars to deal with all calls for assistance was discouraged and a greater proportion of these calls was expected to be dealt with by area beat officers. Finally, greater teamwork between specialist and uniform officers was encouraged by increased joint working, including some joint patrolling.

The evaluation

The main aim of the evaluation of the Havant scheme seems to have been to document the extent to which the redeployment of officers and reassignment of work occurred in practice. On these measures, the scheme was a success. Three months into it, vehicle mileage had dropped by one-quarter, while the number of foot and cycle patrol officers on duty had doubled. In addition, in the first six months, foot and cycle patrol officers dealt with one-quarter of the calls for assistance — several times more than had previously been the case (ibid., Figs. 6.1, 5.2 and 3.2).

Apart from these changes in deployment, there is little available material from which to judge whether the Havant scheme achieved its aims. Whether better supervision of constables or increased cooperation between uniform and specialist officers was achieved remain open questions. Public reactions to the scheme were not sought, nor were any measures taken of the extent to which area beat officers achieved those 'closer contacts with the community' which were expected. Despite this, the scheme has now been extended force-wide. In addition, attempts are being made by Hampshire Constabulary to ensure that foot and cycle officers' time is planned and organised around 'the basic skills of managing a beat in order to use the available time constructively to the best advantage of the public' (ibid., para. 7.2). But no data are at present available from which it is possible to assess whether this aim has been achieved.

The Skelmersdale coordinated policing project

One of the best known experiments in balancing the requirements of response and preventive patrolling is the Skelmersdale coordinated policing experiment set up by the Lancashire Constabulary in 1979. The scheme was preceded by a survey of patrol constables and their sergeants, who reported being overburdened with paperwork and unhappy at being unable to build lasting relationships with the public. Eighty per cent of them never worked more than four consecutive days on any one beat (Laugharne, 1982).

The main purpose of the scheme was to provide a better service to the community, by enabling patrol officers to establish and develop sustained relationships with the public. It had three main aims:

> to determine the capability of the uniform section patrol to carry out preventive policing;
> to maintain an adequate emergency response; and
> to achieve flexibility in order to re-deploy resources to achieve specific objectives without long term detriment to the above (Lancashire Constabulary Memorandum, quoted in Brown, 1981).

Officers were released for preventive patrol in two ways. First, a computerised incident logging system was introduced to replace the old system of written reports. This cut down officers' paperwork by 70 per cent, thus releasing them for operational duties. Second, existing officers (ten sergeants and 60 constables) were redeployed into two groups, with rather over half of them (six sergeants and 34 constables) providing emergency response and the remainder committed to structured (or preventive) patrol. The structured patrol (four sergeants and 26 constables) was organised into four area teams, each responsible for policing a different part of the town, on foot and in three flexible shifts.

The Skelmersdale scheme has been highly acclaimed (Brown, 1981) and other forces have adopted parts of it or modifications of it.[6] It was evaluated both by the Lancashire force (Yates, 1981) and independently (Brown, 1981).[7] The evaluation is worth dealing with in some detail because it typifies what seems to have become a standard approach to the evaluation of special policing projects with some important implications for how those initiatives are debated and discussed (see Weatheritt, 1983).

Brown collected information on crime and on patterns of deployment and he talked to police officers involved in the scheme and some of the people who lived and worked in Skelmersdale. He tested each of the three aims of the scheme (see above) against these data and found that they had all been fulfilled. The ability of the police to respond to emergency calls did not seem to have been adversely affected by the experiment: on the contrary it increased the availability of manpower, especially at times of greatest demand. Moreover, most officers seemed happy with the situation and reported only 'occasional inadequacies' in response capacity (Brown, 1981, p. 5), despite the fact that the scheme saved around 37,000 car miles a year (Laugharne, 1982, p. 6). In addition, Brown found that the ready availability of information from the incident logging system on the types of incidents the police dealt with helped them to assess their workload better and to plan a more flexible response to it.

Brown devotes most of his report to what he describes as 'the centrepiece' of the experiment — the work of the structured patrols. He notes the drop in reported crime in Skelmersdale during the course of the experiment (crime elsewhere in the Lancashire Constabulary area rose) and an increase in the detection rate several times higher than that for the rest of the force. Although he fails to make the link explicit, the reader is nevertheless led to infer that these improvements resulted from the work of the structured patrols. According to Brown, structured patrol officers were able to maintain 'a constant deterrent presence', helped 'create, strengthen and sustain local networks . . . of care and order' and 'by using information given by and gathered from the community helped detect local crime and apprehend local offenders' (Brown, p. 11).

Brown's account is rich in examples of how these effects were achieved and unlike most police patrol studies conveys a strong sense of how structured patrol officers spent their time, how they felt about their work and how other people — their colleagues and members of the public — felt about them. The overwhelming impression (relieved only by some less than adulatory comments by response officers) is of a group of officers dedicated to their work, admired and trusted by local people and able to use that trust in the cooperative task of preventing crime, detecting offenders and maintaining order. Brown writes that the contacts that these officers made with the public in 'allaying anxieties and fears, restoring confidence [and] breeding security . . . serve to strengthen trust in and contact with the police and stimulate fresh flows of information for both the prevention and detection of crime' (p. 10). Officers required to work their beats rather than just respond to incidents also changed their perspectives on the nature of the policing task, so that 'the more a PC becomes involved in the life of an area, the more likely he is to shift from short-term to long-term perspectives on his functions, and from unilateral ''law enforcement'' methods of policing to greater use of informal collaborative methods aimed at long-term preventive and ''peace keeping'' objectives' (p. 8). The change in outlook Brown identifies was not only a practical and pragmatic one but also a moral one. He writes of the patrol sergeants, for example, that they

> have become, in effect, mini Chief Constables of their own areas, growing in understanding, leadership qualities, job satisfaction and community reputation, essentially makers rather than doers of the police job. And it is clear that each has grown with the job, both in police responsibility and public accountability, and that each of them acts with ever growing confidence and autonomy (p. 12).

Although the work of the structured patrol officers wins his virtually unqualified approval (he describes the Skelmersdale experiment as a 'model' system of policing), Brown acknowledges that there were many problems with the scheme. Despite the impression he gives of an unceasing round of purposeful and constructive activity, a large minority of structured patrol officers are reported as being bored with the humdrum nature of their jobs and missing the sense of camaraderie and group solidarity engendered by shift work. Structured patrol work also tended to attract the least experienced officers (p. 12) and it proved difficult to integrate their work with that of the response teams. In effect, says Brown, two teams of officers existed, operating in both practical and ideological isolation from one another, and demonstrating

> very palpably a gap in ideology as to the very nature of policing. Just as response work in cars tends to shape 'enforcers of the law', so area work on foot tends to shape 'keepers of the peace': . . . this ideological issue divides the police service on a national scale (p. 21).

It is clear that, just as Brown regards law enforcement as the current dominant ideology and style of policing, so he also wishes to elevate peace-keeping to hegemonic status.

Many of the problems identified by Brown have been documented elsewhere (see, for example, Jones 1980). But because of his concern to counter what he represents as the entirely negative effects of response policing on police ideology and practice and because of an undisguised preference for the kind of policing style and policing persona that structured patrol officers represent, Brown ends up by evangelising on their behalf rather than critically evaluating their work. He selects evidence to suit his case and overlooks inconsistencies and ambiguities in his data. In doing so he helps to contribute to the ideological gap he identifies.

The most important omission is his failure to say anything constructive about response officers' work, or even to describe what they did. The establishment and maintenance of good police-public relations in Skelmersdale is attributed entirely to the efforts of the structured patrols; response officers are ignored. But although they remain invisible in concrete terms, response officers are all too palpable in symbolic ones. They are held responsible for formal, unilateral methods of law enforcement, responding to people as social stereotypes rather than individuals. In contrasting this style (for which he produces almost no concrete evidence) with that of structured patrols, Brown manages to imply that response officers failed to meet public expectations and damaged good police-public relations. There is no evidence that they did so. Indeed, the findings of a study by Ekblom and Heal (1982) of how the police respond to calls from members of the public suggest, on the contrary, that response policing is highly valued by the public and strongly contributes to good police-public relations.

Brown also overestimates the visibility of structured patrols, the amount of contact they had with the public and the public's response to them. His claim that they were able to maintain a 'constant deterrent presence' is belied by the ratio of officers to population. At any one time there was on duty only one officer per 5,000 population (p. 17). The impression he gives of a caring police, getting to know everyone and being admired and respected by the 'whole community' may well be an artefact of the people to whom he spoke. Brown does not vouchsafe the size and composition of his sample, but to judge from the comments he reports it was biased towards people with a relatively high community profile: shopkeepers, a publican, a head teacher, a youth worker and a social worker. Such people are both an extremely small sample of the general population and a highly unrepresentative one: they are precisely the kinds of people that a structured patrol officer would be expected to get to know. At the very least it seems a little unwise to infer widespread community support for police from what these few respondents said.

Brown is also inconsistent in his use of crime figures. Recorded crime reflects not only the incidence of crime but also the extent to which people choose to report it and the way in which the police then record reported events. All three may vary independently of one another and changes in recorded crime may reflect changes in either incidence, reporting or recording rates, or in more than one of them. (Crime or victim surveys are increasingly being used to help separate out these effects and to identify changes in the incidence of crime.)

Brown used changes in recorded crime to help him assess the effects of the new patrolling methods. He documents a number of changes during the first nine months of the scheme. Overall crime rates fell (by 4 per cent), a decrease which was especially marked in the case of burglary which fell by 22 per cent. Detection rates rose, both for crime as a whole (by 8 per cent) and for burglary (by 7 per cent). Brown strongly implies that these changes were due to the presence of structured patrols (see also Laugharne, who writes of 'encouraging trends'). However, his belief in the value of recorded crime statistics begins to falter when he is faced with the figures for criminal damage. These rose by 33 per cent over the same period, an inconvenient fact which Brown immediately neutralises by the discovery that such figures only serve to point to the futility of criminal statistics in this sphere (p. 4). It is hard to disagree with this statement, but it follows from it that the Skelmersdale crime statistics tell us very little about the effect of the experiment on the prevention and detection of crime.

The kind of research that was done on it makes it difficult for an outside observer to judge the effectiveness of the Skelmersdale experiment. Brown's study fulfils certain purposes — for example it acts as a fairly powerful (and, within its limits, persuasive) means of legitimating a particular policing method and policing style. It is not, however, possible to claim that Brown's report is an objective evaluation of the Skelmersdale scheme, since his enthusiasm for it coloured his choice of method and the collection and interpretation of data. It is therefore of interest that the Skelmersdale scheme has been repeated in another force and that considerable stress was put on subjecting it to rigorous evaluation. The results are described in detail below.

The Chelmsley Wood policing experiment and the Police Effectiveness Evaluation Panel

In 1981 a group of four chief constables got together with the Home Office to think about ways of assessing police effectiveness. They decided to replicate the Skelmersdale policing experiment in another force and to evaluate the results. From this partnership grew PEEP — the Police Effectiveness Evaluation Panel — a group of six senior police officers from the forces of Cleveland, Lancashire, North Wales, the West Midlands and Wiltshire and from the Metropolitan Police plus four officials from the Home Office Scientific Research and Development Branch and two from PRSU. The chief constable of the West Midlands offered his force as a site for the replication, which began in 1982 in Chelmsley Wood and ran for just over one year.

PEEP's job was to devise a framework which could be used to evaluate any policing experiment but which, in the first instance, was to be tried out in relation to Chelmsley Wood. Thus not only was the Chelmsley Wood policing scheme to be seen as an experiment, so was the method and approach of its evaluation.

The germ of PEEP was a 1977 Home Office review of preventive policing projects in seven forces,[8] which included a look at how they were being evaluated and whether or not the Home Office could contribute to this process. Having visited each force, Home Office officials concluded that if any serious evaluation of what they had seen was to occur, a central initiative would be necessary. They identified two major areas of concern on which forces would welcome research and where the Home Office would be keen to offer help and perhaps also act as a catalyst in stimulating innovation. These were: how 'reactive' police work could be reorganised so as to yield the largest amount of time for preventive policing; and the effects of different levels and styles of patrol. Both these concerns had formed a major part of the Skelmersdale experiment and were to be repeated in the Chelmsley Wood initiative.

The experiment

PEEP identified 12 essential features of the Skelmersdale scheme, ranging from the use of a microcomputer to log incidents, to increased foot patrol and to the split between response and structured patrols (Scientific Research and Development Branch, 1984b, pp. 12–14). Not all of these features could be replicated in Chelmsley Wood. For example, the West Midlands Police already had a centralised incident logging system and there seemed little point in duplicating it locally. The scope for the large reductions in paperwork achieved under the Skelmersdale scheme, an important benefit to officers involved in it, did not therefore exist in Chelmsley Wood. (Indeed, patrol officers' paperwork actually increased during the course of the experiment when patrol officers took over responsibility from the CID for investigating minor crimes.) Also different in Chelmsley Wood was the existing system of policing. Before the new system, officers in Skelmersdale had patrolled entirely by car. In Chelmsley Wood, by contrast, a form of split policing already existed, with 44 response officers (24 of whom patrolled by car and 20 on foot) and ten resident beat officers (who had duties roughly equivalent to those of Skelmersdale's structured patrols). Overall, the balance in favour of foot patrol was more marked in Chelmsley Wood before the experiment than it had been in Skelmersdale during the experiment.[9]

In the event, the redeployment of officers at Chelmsley Wood involved little change in the balance between vehicle patrols and foot patrols. Instead, existing foot patrol officers were reorganised, together with the resident beat officers, into three structured patrols each with responsibility for policing a newly created structured patrol area. Twenty-eight constables were redeployed in this way, response cover being maintained by 30 constables who patrolled by car.

The evaluation philosophy

The most innovatory feature of PEEP was its aim to develop a model for evaluating policing schemes that would have general application. The panel sought to find a middle way between what SRDB identified as two contrasting research styles: costly experiments carefully designed to test specific hypotheses, which took a long time to produce results, seemed to satisfy nobody but the experimenters and which no-one else took any notice of; and entirely subjective assessments aimed more at vindicating what was done than at drawing lessons from it. SRDB's judicious feeling was that in order to perform research into police effectiveness that would be 'timely, conclusive and persuasive to chief constable and academic researcher alike, a new kind of evaluative methodology had to be developed from an amalgam of police experience and scientific objectivity' (ibid., p. 4). PEEP was to provide the police experience, SRDB the scientific objectivity.

PEEP began by trying to define the objectives of the Chelmsley Wood scheme, a process described in the SRDB report as a necessary precondition of rigorous evaluation. A list of 700 possible objectives was produced which was eventually whittled down by the panel via a lengthy and time-consuming process to 125 objectives on which they were unanimously agreed. From this list, ten 'basis objectives' (see Appendix A) were identified. These formed the basis of a hierarchically arranged tree depicting all the agreed objectives, which extends over 29 pages of SRDB's report.

Information expected to be relevant to the objectives was collected by SRDB. It included deployment statistics; crime statistics, including information on how crimes were reported; information on complaints; and information from incident logs. In addition, the West Midlands Police undertook surveys of the public in Chelmsley Wood and of the police officers involved in the scheme, both before it was implemented and after it had been running for some time. The final assessment of whether the objectives of the experiment had been achieved was undertaken by PEEP itself, using the objectives tree and the data that had been collected to be relevant to those objectives.

The findings

In terms of operational policing, the Chelmsley Wood policing project was not on balance a success. On the plus side, the scheme was successful in achieving the redeployment of officers from response duties to structured patrol while maintaining adequate response cover, and in achieving greater flexibility of deployment. Also, although the level of foot patrols did not increase overall, the scheme succeeded in getting one or two additional officers out on the streets during the day and reducing coverage at night. Set against these gains were the facts that supervision failed to improve (and in the case of probationary constables deteriorated), teamwork decreased, there was no significant reduction in specialist roles and paperwork was not reduced. Finally, although the aim of making more officers responsible for a single area had been achieved, the amount of time these officers actually spent in those areas declined (see Butler and Tharme, 1983, Table 6 and p. 97).

Where PEEP identified particular effects (whether positive or negative), it went on to look at their implications, particularly in terms of the nature, purpose and results of contacts between police officers and members of the public. Although it lacked data to answer many of the questions it posed, the information that was available has a bearing on the questions about the efficiency of foot patrol which are largely or entirely absent from other studies.

In marked contrast to what Brown claimed for Skelmersdale, the introduction of structured patrolling in Chelmsley Wood had little effect on public perceptions of policing, people's feelings of safety, or the ability of the police to prevent and detect crime. Officers did not develop a better knowledge of local people, problems and crime. They spent no more time under the new scheme making contact with people than they had done before and the number of visits to youth clubs, community groups and residents' meetings actually declined — by 60 per cent. The visibility of patrolling police did not improve and less time was spent in preventive patrol and in carrying out basic crime prevention such as checking properties and suspicious persons. Finally, crime rose during the experiment. The public survey found a 5 per cent overall increase in reported levels of victimisation and the incidence of burglaries almost doubled.

The lessons of Chelmsley Wood

In retrospect, it is obvious that the choice of Chelmsley Wood as a replication site for the Skelmersdale experiment was likely to work against the success of structured patrol. Well-established relationships between police and public already existed in Chelmsley Wood. There was no evidence that these relationships were wanting and there is no indication in SRDB's report of how the formation of structured patrols might have been expected to improve on existing relationships — one of the main aims of structured patrols in Skelmersdale. (If anything, structured patrols might have been expected to disrupt existing relationships by severing existing links between individual resident beat officers and small beat areas.) In short, despite SRDB's strictures against the misapplication of scientific methods to policing experiments, there appears to have been no rationale for the Chelmsley Wood experiment other than the wish to replicate the Skelmersdale initiative and the fact that a site was available in Chelmsley Wood.

Despite this major difficulty, there are lessons of wider application to be drawn from Chelmsley Wood both for policing and for policing evaluation.

First, Chelmsley Wood showed that it is possible to run a policing experiment which fails to fulfil its objectives and to admit that this is the case: indeed it is in the nature of an experiment that this possibility is entertained. The purpose of an experiment is to test hypotheses about what might be the case, not to seek justification of what was done. In policing experiments, where the rhetoric of change is often used to obscure what actually happens, it is important that this lesson be faced head on and it is worth remarking upon that those involved in evaluating Chelmsley Wood did so. Their findings, particularly those relating to the supposed superiority and visibility of foot patrols, inject a refreshing note of scepticism into an area of policing policy where assumptions are so deeply held that they have become virtually closed off from debate. If the Chelmsley Wood 'model' of evaluation is applied to other policing initiatives — as it is intended it should be[10] — this should help to improve the quality of information available to the police about their own activity as well as the quality of their internal debate about it.

The second lesson relates to policing. Chelmsley Wood demonstrated that a policy focusing on foot patrol does not by itself lead to better policing. Many of the officers involved in the experiment were unclear about what the experimental changes were supposed to achieve. In particular, the aims of the experiment do not seem to have been conveyed in ways which would help officers plan specific and appropriate strategies and styles. In this respect, Chelmsley Wood did no more than repeat one of the more widespread and unsatisfactory features of other patrol experiments — and indeed patrol itself.

In essence the failure — exemplified in an uncharacteristically honest fashion by Chelmsley Wood — has been to ask fundamental questions about what officers should be doing on patrol, whether or not they are doing a good job there, and how those to whom they are accountable can know this. For experimental and indeed for policing purposes these general questions need to be broken down and given detailed and highly specific content.

Several forces have begun to grapple with this undoubtedly difficult task. The West Midlands Police, for example, have produced a detailed analysis of what the force permanent beat officers do and have considered in some depth what they should do. The latter is of particular interest since it concludes, against the prevailing orthodoxy of 'community policing', that the permanent beat officer should 'primarily concern himself with crime and criminals'. The Metropolitan Police as part of its neighbourhood policing experiment has set out to encourage beat officers to think in highly specific terms about the problems on their beats and to develop appropriate ways of tackling them. It is also centrally concerned to develop means by which supervising officers can judge the effectiveness of patrol officers. Such an approach, known as 'directed patrol', aims to instil a sense of purpose into officers' activities. Most important, it involves considering the ends of policing as well as — and before — the means by which they are to be achieved.

It will be some time before the lessons — whatever they may be — from these and other similar departures are available to be absorbed. For the moment, all that can be said is that they provide some evidence of a new more fruitful scepticism about the value of policing activity. Such scepticism is important if the empirical ethic is to temper the moral idealism which has in the past characterised much research, not just into patrolling, but also into other policing activities that bring officers into contact with the public. One such activity is crime prevention, and I deal with this in the following two chapters.

Notes

1. No national figures are published on the proportion of force strength assigned to patrol. It is probably about 40 per cent (Hough, 1980, p. 7). A similar figure is given for the Metropolitan Police in one of the Policy Studies Institute reports on the force (Smith, 1983, vol. III, Table III.I).

2. *Parliamentary Debates, Commons*, vol. 813, col. 367.

3. The Edmund Davies committee recommended an immediate increase (from 1978) in police pay of 40 per cent and subsequent annual increases in line with average earnings (HMSO, 1978). Between 1978 and 1984 police pay rose by 140 per cent.

4. The background papers prepared by the Metropolitan Police in connection with the force's neighbourhood policing experiment (see Appendix A) postulate a 'reactive spiral' which goes as follows. Committing resources to response work means fewer officers to carry out preventive work. Less prevention means more crime and disorder, which in turn increases public demand for more reaction. The amount of police time spent on reactive work thus increases; and the reactive spiral takes another turn. The neighbourhood policing strategy is aimed at breaking this spiral. See Beckett and Hart, 1981.

5. My account is a more critical one than that given by the West Midlands Police (1982), which is rather more committed to demonstrating the success of the experiments. My account is based on some re-analysis and reinterpretation of West Midlands Police data.

6. For example, the Havant policing scheme described above initially used the incident logging system devised for Skelmersdale although it has since been abandoned.

7. For practical purposes these two evaluations are not readily distinguishable from one another. Brown draws on much of Yates' data plus his own observations of the scheme in action. In the ensuing discussion I refer only to Brown's report, because it is the shorter of the two and is easier to obtain.

8. The Home Office found considerable differences in the willingness of forces to define preventive policing and in the way in which they did so. These differences are reflected in the disparate range of projects that the Home Office visitors examined. These were: Devon and Cornwall (Police Advisory Telephone Service and the Juvenile Bureau); Greater Manchester (Community Contact Branch); the West Midlands (Handsworth, The Bolton Estate, The Castle Vale Estate); and West Yorkshire (reallocation of manpower according to workload). For its part, the Home Office defined preventive policing as: 'the positive deployment of police resources not required for immediate response to public demand and other unavoidable commitments'.

9. In Chelmsley Wood, 56 per cent of constables patrolled on foot before the experiment and 44 per cent by car. In Skelmersdale, during the experiment, 43 per cent of constables were assigned to foot patrol, 57 per cent to vehicle patrol.

10. If there is any criticism to be made of the SRDB evaluation, it is that it is over-complex and over-systematised. Twenty-nine-page objective trees are more likely to provoke intellectual fatigue amongst potential evaluators than to whet their intellectual appetites.

4 CRIME PREVENTION IN THEORY

The Home Secretary hopes that the opportunity afforded by the introduction of new methods of beat patrolling will be taken to stress the important part which 'area' constables can play in preventing crime. But crime prevention is not the responsibility of the police alone. It is a cooperative effort in which every part of the community is involved. (Home Office circular, *Crime Prevention*, issued in May 1968).

The Government has already taken steps to strengthen and equip the police, and the police have responded effectively. But effective crime prevention requires more than police action alone. It demands a comprehensive approach which attracts a strong measure of public support and which rests on a foundation of close collaboration. (The Lord Elton, Parliamentary Under Secretary of State at the Home Office, November 1982 (Home Office, 1983d).)

Fifteen years separate these two statements of policy intent. Exhortations for 'the community as a whole' to be involved in crime prevention, far from marking a significant break or step on from past policies,[1] have been a central plank of government thinking for some time. In this chapter I explore how the wish to make crime prevention a cooperative enterprise has been translated into institutions for keeping crime prevention in the public eye; and at how the theory of crime prevention and its relationships to practice have developed over the last twenty years. Ideas of community and cooperative effort are readily invoked as sources of inspiration, but there seem to have been persistent difficulties in translating them into concrete and effective action. The development of crime prevention in the police service is marked more by a series of obstacles to success than by a history of achievements. This fact has implications for the future — for it is easy, and often convenient, for those who are professionally committed to encouraging more, and more effective prevention, to overlook or play down the difficulties in achieving it.

The past few years have seen considerable growth in attempts to raise and expand crime prevention consciousness within the police service and outside it. Official disappointment with past performance

44

has led to a fresh look at what the limits to effective action are. Much thought has been put into how those limits might be extended, particularly by means which also promise to generate community support for police. For despite the importance that has officially been attached to it, crime prevention has traditionally been something of a Cinderella amongst police specialisms. It is currently being injected with a new dose of rhetorical vigour and a commitment to practical action: new optimisms are being fashioned to help brighten the slightly tarnished image of the old ones. This initiative, which has come largely from central government, is described later in this chapter. It is too early to say what sorts of effects it will have and as a result, much of what is described here marks only an intermediate stage in a much longer process of trying to create enthusiasm and commitment to action amongst those with influence in getting things done.

It is a commonplace of policing that it is the primary duty of every police officer to prevent crime. For some officers — the 500 or so specialist crime prevention officers — preventing crime is their sole duty. The aims, organisational form and supporting institutions of this specialist service were established in the mid-1960s following the recommendations of the Cornish Committee on the Prevention and Detection of Crime, which reported 20 years ago (Home Office, 1965). At that time, the idea that crime prevention was a subject in its own right, with a separate claim on resources, was beginning to take root and a few forces had established small crime prevention departments. Taking its cue from these developments, the Cornish Committee argued that specialist officers were needed to keep abreast of developments in the technology of crime prevention; to bring a more professional approach than had existed hitherto to the design and dissemination of publicity material; and to 'strive constantly' to build and maintain relationships with organisations outside the police service in order to impress on them the importance of their own responsibilities in preventing crime. The Committee recommended that an officer of at least inspector rank be appointed in each force as its crime prevention officer, with sergeants on each division to carry out local crime prevention surveys and liaise with patrol constables.

Although crime prevention officers were to be distinguished from other officers by the nature of their specialist duties, the Cornish Committee was very aware of the dangers of seeming to shunt crime prevention into a specialist backwater. 'We consider it vital that any crime prevention organisation should not diminish the responsibility of other members of the force towards crime prevention' (para. 214). 'Possibly the most important yet neglected aspect of crime prevention is the need to stimulate and maintain an interest amongst all members of the force' (para. 211). One of the most important functions of crime prevention officers was to do this. They were to lecture regularly at recruit training and refresher courses and to work closely with force training officers; to circulate information to patrol officers on crime trends and active criminals; and to solicit from patrol officers crime prevention suggestions and information about crimes and activities on their beats. Moreover, beat (and CID) officers were to continue to be 'the main source' of crime prevention advice to the public with most simple crime prevention surveys remaining in the hands of non-specialists.

The Committee felt that crime prevention was not only a matter for the police service, but for other organisations too. It made its sentiments clear from the outset in asserting that 'The prevention of crime needs the work and cooperation of many elements in society.' In the same optimistic and exhortatory spirit which characterises much of current discussion, the Committee took note that the past few years had seen 'an increasing awareness of the community's responsibilities towards crime prevention' but that constant effort was needed to overcome apathy, generate interest and translate that interest into practical effort. The Committee itself had discussions with architects, with the Post Office, and with banks and insurance companies about the kinds of initiatives these organisations ought to be taking. It recommended that this work be built on and extended to other organisations: motor manufacturers, the Road Haulage Association, the building trade, retail traders, local authorities, the British Standards Institution and welfare organisations; and that a central advisory body should take on the job of liaison and persuasion. This body was to have both coordinating and declaratory functions. It would pool material on local initiatives, coordinate national publicity campaigns and liaise with other interests. In other words it would stand as evidence of the police service's commitment to crime prevention and its willingness to apply that commitment to generating practical activity.

If crime prevention was to become a specialism, crime prevention officers would need to be trained. The Committee recommended short courses, based at an existing force training school and organised and run by a course director and two instructors, each on secondment from the police service. They were to be supplemented by civilian lecturers on specialist subjects. The syllabus recommended by the Committee covered the hardware and equipment of crime prevention; protection of premises, including those presenting special risks; inspection of premises; liaison with architects, insurance surveyors, the fire service and other organisations; vehicle security; the education of beat colleagues; and publicity and propaganda. By the time the Committee reported, the Home Office Crime Prevention Centre at Stafford had been set up and had begun to accept students and to teach the kinds of courses recommended in the Committee's report.

With some changes of emphasis, the Cornish Committee's recommendations set a framework and tone for the establishment of a crime prevention service which has remained virtually unchanged since it reported. The specialist crime prevention service remains much as the Committee envisaged: one or two headquarters' officers and an officer on each division, who organise exhibitions, give talks and survey domestic and commercial premises to make recommendations about appropriate security measures. Specialist training courses are provided by the Home Office Crime Prevention Centre at Stafford and although these courses have been expanded to take in more officers and cover more subjects, the Centre can still boast that 'many of the subjects in the first programme are still taught and form the basis of the course' (Home Office Crime Prevention Centre, 1983).

The other main string to the Cornish Committee's bow, a central advisory body to stand as official affirmation of the importance of crime prevention, and to coordinate, cajole and liaise with a variety of interested parties, was formed in 1967 as the Home Office Standing Committee on Crime Prevention. The Standing Committee's terms of reference are to 'bring together persons and organisations who have a common interest in crime prevention for an exchange of ideas and a stimulus to further effort'. The people chosen to represent these common interests were from industry and commerce, central government and the police.[2]

The early work of the Standing Committee was concerned with three main issues. First, it developed a series of national and regional crime prevention publicity campaigns, which continue today. Second, it appointed two sub-committees, one on static property (that is, commercial and domestic premises) and one on mobile property (vehicles), which were to be primarily concerned with the protection of property through physical security. Over the years, publicity (particularly the annual Home Office crime prevention campaigns) and the physical security concerns of its two sub-committees have dominated the Standing Committee's agenda. (It meets twice a year.) Finally, the Committee was anxious to find some way of duplicating at a local level the philosophy behind its work and, in particular, to enlist local community support in preventing crime. To this end it recommended the setting up of crime prevention panels in all towns with a population of more than 150,000.

Crime prevention panels

Until recently, when attention has also begun to be paid to the mobilising potential of neighbourhood watch and the new police/community consultative arrangements, crime prevention panels have been 'the means recommended by the Home Office by which members of the community voluntarily help the police prevent crime' (Home Office, 1978a). The first panels were set up in the mid-1960s as a way of promoting and harnessing local preventive effort, with a Home Office circular, issued in 1968, providing a catalyst to development. Although the Home Office has made its views clear on the desirability of crime prevention panels, it has been left to individual forces to decide whether or not to establish them. As a result, some forces are well-endowed with panels, others have few or none. There are currently around 200 of them. Panels' membership follows broadly similar lines to that of the Home Office Standing Committee on Crime Prevention but with a local emphasis and many local variations. Local business and commercial interests including the press, and voluntary and professional organisations are likely to be well represented, the statutory services less so. In a survey it conducted in 1970 of the organisation and work of panels, the Home Office found that virtually all of them were chaired by the police who also exercised a strong influence over membership (Home Office, 1971).

Panels have no formal status. Their terms of reference are to examine proposals on crime prevention made by the police, panel members and members of the public and to help disseminate crime prevention propaganda (Home Office, 1968a). The traditional emphasis of their work has been on running publicity campaigns and on the importance of physical security, an emphasis which is very similar to that followed by force crime prevention departments. Panels have helped to fund and carry out property-marking schemes and the fitting of simple security devices, such as door chains, to elderly people's homes. Panel initiatives are regularly reported in *Crime Prevention News*.

Panels' work varies considerably in quality and vigour but very little is known about its effectiveness. The Home Office has advised that in the absence of any proof of the success of their work, panels should persevere in their efforts, have faith in what they are doing and show a willingness to experiment with enthusiasm (sic) (Home Office, 1978a). Such advice suggests that whatever the cost effectiveness of panels' work, they are seen as a useful way of demonstrating that something is being done. Panels are also regarded as a vehicle for promoting good police-public relations.

What is wrong with crime prevention?

Two histories of crime prevention can be written. There is the one of official reports and statements, the elevation of crime preventive objectives to be the primary purpose of policing, and the development of organisations and institutions for thinking about crime prevention and instigating action. Looked at from this perspective, the history is an encouraging one: not only does crime prevention receive strong rhetorical support, it also appears to rest on a sound base of institutional deliberation and activity.

The other history of crime prevention goes behind the statements of intention to look at how far and in what ways preventive objectives have become part of day-to-day policing; on the relationship of crime prevention specialists to the rest of the police service; on what crime prevention officers do and how useful and effective this is; and on how knowledge of what works and what is less successful is made known to crime prevention officers and diffused throughout the police service. On these criteria, the achievements are less impressive. Crime prevention has not become part of mainstream policing and the specialist crime prevention service has been left to languish in something of a policing backwater. There is evidence that a lot of specialist crime prevention work fails to make an impact. The arrangements for identifying and disseminating 'good practice' within the police service are rudimentary. Whatever the expressed commitment of senior police officers and successive governments to the view that prevention is the primary object of policing, the crime prevention job remains an activity performed on the sidelines while the main action takes place elsewhere.

One measure of the importance that the police attach to preventive work is the status of the crime prevention service within forces and the way its work is evaluated and rewarded. Crime prevention is not a glamorous specialism: it lacks the aura of prestige which attaches to other specialisms such as the CID.[3] It is also a small specialism: around 500 officers — about one per 115,000 of population and less than 0.5 per cent of total force strength — are committed full time to crime preventive work. (Detectives by contrast make up 12 per cent of force strength.) In addition, the service offers only limited opportunities for career progression. The highest rank that can be attained in crime prevention is that of chief inspector in the larger forces, and inspector in the smaller ones.[4] (Operational heads elsewhere in the police service are normally ranked at chief superintendent.) Crime prevention has traditionally been seen as a relatively undemanding posting for officers who are soon to retire. Until recently, when the figure has fallen to about fifteen years, the average length of service of constables and sergeants attending the basic training course for newly appointed crime prevention officers at the Crime Prevention Centre was 20 years, just five years short of the period at which police officers become eligible for pensionable retirement on half pay.[5]

In view of the current rekindling of interest in crime prevention, it is perhaps also a reflection of its status that there has been so little apparent interest in finding out what crime prevention officers actually do and in the relationship between crime prevention departments and the rest of the force. Except in the Metropolitan Police, the kinds of activity analyses that some forces have carried out on the work of patrol officers, and particularly community constables, have not been applied widely to the work of crime prevention officers. Yet despite their relatively lowly position within the organisational hierarchy, crime prevention officers have been given an ambitious and extensive brief. In 1979, an ACPO working party listed 68 tasks which it thought ought to fall to crime prevention officers (Association of Chief Police Officers, 1979, Appendix D). The working party summarised them as:

a. the cultivation of a working two-way relationship between beat patrol officers and the crime prevention officer, and the encouragement of all officers to report matters of crime prevention interest;

b. the collection, coordination and dissemination of crime prevention information and information on current trends in crime;

c. the acquiring of a thorough knowledge of technical aids to security, by study of appropriate journals and visits to manufacturers of locks, safes etc;

d. the inspection of property where there are special or difficult security features; and the keeping of records of such visits to enable follow-up visits to be made at appropriate times;

e. maintaining a firm relationship with local authorities and all other bodies to whom advice can be given on crime prevention;

f. the giving of talks to local bodies on crime prevention and personal protection, and the giving of advice to householders on request or whenever the opportunity arises;

g. ensuring that crime prevention literature is used to its best effect and displayed or distributed on all appropriate occasions; the crime prevention officer should always have available a collection of physical protection devices for selective display;

h. the regular giving of lectures at probationer and refresher courses and the issue of a crime prevention booklet for the guidance of all members of the force;

i. to support and liaise with other departments of the force in the task of community relations and preventive policing and to co-operate with social agencies concerned with the welfare of children and young persons;

j. to co-operate and liaise with the security industry, and with fire prevention officers, to ensure that security standards do not conflict with fire safety requirements;

k. to give advice on security to builders and architects in the planning stages of buildings, and if necessary survey premises from plans; to maintain liaison with architects and local authority planning departments;

l. to encourage the activities of crime prevention panels;

m. to prepare articles for inclusion in local publications and newspapers in collaboration with the force public relations officer (ibid., pp. 13–14).

Although it has always been envisaged that crime prevention officers should work on a broad front (this is implicit in both the Cornish Committee's prescriptions and in the above job description), in practice their tasks have been defined more selectively and much more narrowly. This is partly a matter of resources, for it is difficult to see how even the most conscientious and diligent of crime prevention departments might do justice to more than a few of the tasks outlined by the ACPO working party.[6] But it is also a matter of philosophy. 'Community-based' approaches to crime prevention have not, on the whole, formed a major part of the tradition of specialist crime prevention. Little attention has been given to how best to build up and maintain the kind of contacts and channels of liaison and communication that 'community' approaches imply. Whatever the expressed importance of these wider aspects of their role, crime prevention officers have in practice become what a recent Home Office report describes as 'primarily physical security experts' (Gladstone, 1980, p. 4), whose source of expertise lies mainly in their knowledge of target hardening measures, rather than in research, liaison and communicative skills.

It is the security aspect of their work which is heavily emphasised in the courses provided by the Crime Prevention Centre. Around two-thirds of the basic course for newly appointed crime prevention officers is devoted to imparting technical knowledge of physical and security hardware, the special security problems posed by certain sorts of premises and by commercial transactions and the problems and methods of security surveying.[7] Since there is much in the way of technical knowledge to be imparted, and some of it is highly specialised, this emphasis is un-surprising. It does however mean that there is little time left over for teaching other topics. In 1983, the four-week basic course of 150 ses-sions contained only ten sessions on subjects related to community liaison.[8] Although the emphasis of the courses for more senior officers is very different (almost all of the four-day course for force crime preven-tion officers, that is inspectors and chief inspectors, is given over to broader aspects of prevention), it is fair to say that, for most crime prevention officers, it is the technology of crime prevention that dominates their formal training and that the emphasis and approach of this training goes hand in hand with the way crime prevention problems are tackled in forces. There is, as yet, relatively little in the training they receive that indicates that involving the community in crime prevention is expected to occupy much of crime prevention officers' attention, let alone form the main focus of their approach.

In 1979, the Association of Chief Police Officers set up a working party to look at what the Centre's role should be and whether the courses it provided were adequate preparation for the job of preventing crime. The working party defined the Centre's aims as follows:

> To train officers in crime prevention skills; to keep abreast of technological developments in crime prevention equipment and methods by liaising with industry and other agencies; to co-ordinate and disseminate information on crime prevention measures to the British police service, and to industry and other agencies; to develop new techniques; and to crystallize thoughts on crime prevention ac-tivities and policies (para. 3.1).

The working party looked at the content and balance of the courses being offered and examined the case for changing their emphasis slight-ly by introducing crime prevention officers to what it called 'preventive policing' or 'community policing' approaches to crime prevention. (It did not define what it meant by these terms.) But although the working party remained non-committal as to the value of such approaches, it did not think that crime prevention officers undergoing basic training should be taught much about them. It preferred the *status quo* and stressed the need for the Centre to concentrate on the physical aspects of crime prevention.

Whatever the intentions of the Working Party, one effect of its recommendations has been to endorse the confinement of crime prevention officers' work to a security ghetto. Given the attempts described below to increase the status and profile of crime prevention, the current director of the Centre feels hamstrung by the Working Party's limited expectations of it. He would like to broaden the Centre's approach and revamp its courses to put more stress on communicating the crime prevention message and on community-oriented approaches to prevention, as well as to tie what is taught more closely to available research. (The basic course, for example, contains little on research findings, despite their clear implications for changes in practice.) Training institutions are normally regarded at the very least as instruments of new policies and at best as being at the cutting edge of change. Yet the Centre's current resources, its small staff, the expectations which attach to it and the demands which have been made of it all mean that it has been unable to undertake any fundamental reappraisal of its role or the value and relevance of the courses it offers. At the time of writing, the Centre's work is being reviewed by a further working party which is expected to publish a report in 1985. It seems fair to comment that without some radical reappraising, crime prevention officers are unlikely to become fully accredited ambassadors for broadly-based preventive policies.

Measuring the effectiveness of crime prevention

Many police officers do not believe the effectiveness of crime prevention can be measured and in terms of the types of day-to-day accounting normally applied to police work they are right. Crime prevention officers are not in the business of getting 'results' in the conventional sense of detections and arrests. The results of crime prevention are invisible. A prevented crime is one that does not occur; an effective crime prevention programme is a set of strategies that maximises that occurrence of non-events. There is, literally, nothing to show for successful crime prevention. In an organisation where immediate (and even longer term) rewards lie in making things happen, those who wish to demonstrate the importance of crime prevention start with a distinct disadvantage. Political statements which seek to improve the status of crime prevention simply by reiterating how important it is, have tended to omit the fact that prevention does not generate immediate practical results: rather different kinds of criteria to those normally adopted in policing are therefore required to judge how far prevention is achieving its aims.

Police forces have been slow to devise such criteria. With a few exceptions, the effects of crime prevention departments' activities have either been ignored or have been taken for granted. As a result, the assumptions on which most crime prevention is based have changed very little since the Cornish Committee reported. The Committee took as axiomatic, first, that making property more secure protects it from theft or damage; and second, that if people are given authoritative-sounding practical advice about what to do to protect themselves and their property, they will follow it. Hence crime prevention officers' activities traditionally have been organised around finding out what security measures are best suited to the job in hand and then telling people to use them, either through blanket publicity campaigns aimed at large audiences, or through more personalised approaches tailored to particular individuals or groups of individuals.

Home Office research on crime prevention

In the mid-1970s, the Home Office Research and Planning Unit began a programme of research which set out to test the assumptions behind police crime prevention initiatives. Many of these studies are reported in *Designing out crime* (Clarke and Mayhew, 1980),[9] which also draws from them policy implications. The Unit's findings have not been very supportive of traditional crime prevention wisdom. In practice, what sounds to be rational and sensible conceals a number of practical difficulties which are hard for traditional strategies to overcome. There are two interrelated problems. The first is to do with people's awareness of risks and their willingness to take action to minimise them; the second is concerned with the persuasive force of propaganda aimed at publicising those risks and encouraging people to take preventive action.

Many people seem to accord low priority to good security. Substantial numbers, for example, leave their cars unlocked when parked in public places: in one recent study, one-fifth of the vehicles checked in a city centre were found to be insecure (reported in Clarke and Mayhew, 1980, p. 105). Nor are people any more likely to secure their houses adequately. Either they do not install security devices in the first place, or, if they do, they are less than diligent about using them. In a recent study of 450 households, 95 per cent were found to have either partial or poor security[10] and in those which did have good security, one-quarter of respondents admitted to not locking up properly on the last occasion they had left their house empty during the day (Winchester and Jackson, 1982). In another study, 60 per cent of a sample of over 300 burglary victims had no locks beyond ordinary spring locks, bolts or window catches prior to being burgled and 41 per cent of the sample said that they frequently went out leaving doors unlocked and windows open.

The large pool of poorly secured property discovered by these studies implies, in theory at least, a large group of potential beneficiaries of crime prevention advice. Both central government and local forces put considerable effort into trying to reach this audience, mainly by running general publicity campaigns aimed at large groups of people who are presumed to have a common interest in reducing their risk of becoming victims of crime. This effort extends from large scale regional and national campaigns on the television network, to leaflets handed out from force crime prevention exhibition stands at local functions or such initiatives as crime prevention quizzes run in local schools (see, for example, *Crime Prevention News* 2/1983, p. 11 and 1/1984, p. 14). These campaigns can reach very large audiences: most people probably recall having seen at some time publicity material urging them to take simple crime prevention precautions.

The evidence that these kinds of publicity drives achieve what is intended for them is, however, less than reassuring. In 1980, two Home Office researchers reviewed existing research on crime prevention publicity and evaluated two television campaigns aimed respectively at reducing vandalism and car theft and a further campaign aimed at reducing car theft through press and poster advertising (Riley and Mayhew, 1980). They concluded that 'crime prevention advertising in the United Kingdom . . . has not been strikingly successful in promoting changes in behaviour likely to lead to a reduction in crime' (ibid., p. 9). People may remember campaign messages and their attitudes to security may change as a result of them, but altered behaviour by no means follows. The message seems to be that general exhortations to be more security-conscious do not work and that what is needed instead is for publicity campaigns to take into account — to a far greater extent than is currently standard practice — how people perceive the risk of becoming a victim, the immediate influences on their behaviour and why and how that behaviour is resistant to change. (See Mayhew, 1985, for elaboration of this argument and a review of relevant research.)

To the extent that they are able to take account of such factors, localised campaigns aimed at highly specific audiences who have a high risk of being victims of crime may stand a greater chance of success than more generalised campaigns have done. Many forces have introduced some of the elements of such an approach into their campaign work. The West Midlands Police, for example, have used boy scouts to circulate information to households on local burglary patterns (see *Police Review*, 5 March 1982), while the Metropolitan Police have aimed much of their campaign effort to reduce street crime in Lambeth specifically at women, who run a greater risk than do men of being victims of such crimes.[11] Neighbourhood watch schemes (discussed in Chapter 5) provide one of the best opportunities for the police to tailor publicity material to both the expressed needs and the actual behaviour of relatively circumscribed groups of people who share a common interest in wanting to prevent certain sorts of crime. It will be interesting to see whether this more intimate approach creates greater consciousness of the importance of physical security measures and greater diligence in their use, than traditional campaigning methods have done.

It is not difficult to see why people fail to respond to pleas to be more security conscious. To begin with, not everyone runs the same risk of being a victim of crime and for a great many people, that risk is low.[12] Secondly, good security can be expensive[13] and those most at risk, for example from burglary (council house dwellers and inner city residents), are often those least able to afford the costs of installing it. In addition, the value of the goods vulnerable to burglary, which in any case may well be insured, may not be sufficient to justify these costs. In the British Crime Survey two-thirds of burglary victims reported a loss of under £100, while of those who experienced greater losses, one-half received insurance compensation. Finally, security can be highly inconvenient and many people clearly give higher priority to avoiding immediate inconvenience than they do to contemplating the more uncertain and rather distant prospect of falling prey to misfortune.

One clear message of the Home Office research is that effective crime prevention strategies demand, if not a complete break with traditional precepts, then at least a rethink about how best to achieve desired results. As a way of doing this, the Home Office Research and Planning Unit has developed what it calls the 'situational' approach to crime prevention, which aims to tailor specific, highly circumscribed crime prevention solutions to specific, highly circumscribed crime prevention problems. Situational prevention is in many ways an extension of what force crime prevention departments have always done, but it differs in eschewing blanket approaches based on traditional assumptions about what works in favour of specific hypothesis-testing, and in substituting a coherent intellectual framework for what, up to now, has been an *ad hoc* pragmatism. One of its main features is its strong research base and its attempt to pull together what are usually presented as two distinct crime prevention approaches: physical prevention and social prevention.

So far I have talked about physical prevention. I now turn to social prevention before going on to describe what situational prevention is and how it has come to dominate certain aspects of crime prevention policy, and to discuss some of the obstacles to getting it more widely accepted and adopted throughout the police service.

Community involvement and social crime prevention

Many people see the failure of traditional crime prevention as only to be expected, because it fails to tackle the 'real' or 'root' causes of crime. On this view, it is not the physical environment which needs to be manipulated, but rather the social conditions and psychological dispositions that create offenders in the first place. What is needed, therefore, is programmes of action which will help change people's attitudes to offending, encourage respect for law and reduce the wish to commit crimes. This idea has been translated into a variety of policing initiatives: schools liaison programmes; police provision of leisure facilities and activities for young people; and programmes aimed at strengthening or reestablishing social integration and the quality of community life.

That the police not only might be able but also ought to do something about the social conditions which give rise to crime, seems to have been adopted by the police as an explicit goal in the 1960s. Its organisational origins are different from those of physical crime prevention. In the mid-1960s, many forces set up community relations departments, initially as a response to what were seen to be the distinctive policing problems posed by ethnic minorities. For various reasons (discussed by Pope, 1976), these departments quickly developed a much wider brief to maintain and improve public relations generally and to develop and sustain contacts with a variety of statutory and voluntary agencies: thus were community relations and community involvement born as new specialisms. At about the same time, forces were also thinking about how they might best influence the behaviour of young people. Schools liaison programmes and juvenile liaison departments were being set up (see Schaffer, 1980, Chs. 2 and 6) as the police responded to the more widely held notion that educating young people and dealing with them informally could be a more appropriate response to actual and potential law-breaking than invoking the law. By the end of the 1960s, the Children and Young Persons Act 1969 gave statutory recognition to what had been a growing practice throughout the decade: police cautioning of juvenile and young offenders as an alternative to taking them to court. The Act also contributed to the police extending and formalising their relationships with other agencies as forces created specialist departments and/or appointed specialist officers to take decisions on how to deal with juvenile offenders. As part of this process the police consulted with the education, probation and social services, all of which have more of a welfare than a law-enforcement approach to the problems of preventing offending.

As formal means of communication have become established between police and other agencies, they have increasingly been used not only to exchange views and information but also to mount joint initiatives. This has been encouraged by central government. In 1978, the Home Office issued a joint circular (with the Department of Health and Social Security, Department of Education and Science and Welsh Office) which both reflected and sought to develop this trend (Home Office, 1978b). The circular (known as the Ditchley circular) said that policing initiatives to do with juveniles had developed piecemeal, in response to a variety of local circumstances and government policies; and that they were therefore unlikely to be as effective as they could be. The circular saw the answer to more effective endeavour in 'improved coordination and joint activity' between police, probation, education and social services. It urged forces not only to improve their liaison machinery but also to set up more joint initiatives, especially community-based ones. A subsequent circular (Home Office, 1980) documents the kinds of projects that resulted. They include schools liaison programmes, initiatives to deal with truancy, inter-agency secondments, youth work and community involvement and development projects.

The inclusion of community development initiatives in the police response to the Ditchley circular marks an interesting development in crime prevention policy which is partly obscured by the neutral administrative language of cooperation and coordination in which the circular is couched. This is the involvement by police (not just as participants, but also as initiators) in programmes which seek to increase community spirit and community solidarity through involvement in community action. The assumption is that such action will both help to reduce crime and create a more favourable climate for the police to operate in. The most articulate police exponent of this point of view is John Alderson. Alderson bases his argument on two assumptions. The first is that formal institutions of criminal justice have failed to prevent and deter crime because the causes of crime lie in factors which criminal justice institutions cannot affect. Other institutions and individuals can, however, affect these factors, so that what is needed to control crime is some way of bringing other people into the enterprise. The second assumption is that it is the mark of a morally superior police to seek to prevent crime. Alderson brings these two assumptions together in the idea that preventive policing 'opens up the entire body politic in the search for causes' (Alderson, 1979, p. 34). He sees the police as not only being in a unique position to identify these causes but also to take action — or persuade others to take action — to deal with them. Alderson is in little doubt that the causes of crime lie in the breakdown of informal community controls. The job of the police therefore is to help reestablish these controls: 'to strengthen that greatest of all prevention, social and mutual trust in communities' (sic) (ibid., p. 39). In order to do this, the police need to take on the role of both moral and practical leadership; where social discipline and trust are lacking, the police should seek to create it. The police are 'particularly well placed' to provide such leadership; to 'penetrate the community in a multitude of ways in order to influence its behaviour from illegality and toward legality' (ibid.).

Alderson's ideas raise controversial issues about what the proper limits are to police action which are only partially illuminated by the available accounts of police-instigated community action I describe in Chapter 5. However, his discussion of preventive policing as an essentially moral project, designed to create a particular ethos of policing and to act as a consensual rallying cry, raises questions of how far it is practicable to submit social prevention initiatives to tests of practical achievements. These questions are explored more fully in relation to particular initiatives in Chapter 5.

Situational crime prevention. Defining a policy and promulgating practice

In 1975 the Home Office set up a Working Group on Crime Prevention, with a brief to look more widely than traditional crime prevention institutions had done at the broad crime prevention field:

> in order to identify the scope for progress in influencing social policy for crime prevention purposes or for articulating the crime prevention dimension to other departments (Home Office, 1976, para. 1).[14]

The Working Group did a number of things. It tried to find some way of reconciling the apparently competing claims of physical and social crime prevention within a framework of action which would appeal to other government departments and involve them in crime prevention initiatives. It looked at the philosophy of crime prevention and its relationship to research and at how research could be used to advance philosophy and practice. And it set out to generate wider interest in crime prevention and to persuade other organisations to get involved in it. Here it was less interested in general exhortation than in trying to get something specific off the ground and to test whether it worked or not.

In recasting crime prevention problems in terms of rational, information-based planning the Working Group's report clearly bears the stamp of its more research-minded members. (In this it presages and closely parallels the policing by objectives approach described in Chapter 8.) The Group reviewed existing social and physical approaches to crime prevention with a view to distilling a new and more effective set of prescriptions from them but was forced to conclude that 'current knowledge of effective crime prevention measures [is] either of too limited a scope or . . . not substantial enough to sustain the broader Home Office initiative envisaged in the terms of reference' (para. 2). The Working Group concluded that

> The Home Office does not have available to it sufficient knowledge about the broader aspects of crime prevention nor has it developed the right sort of intellectual framework to sustain at present a convincing or helpful approach to other departments or agencies on the crime prevention dimension of their policies (para. 10).

The Group's answer to this state of affairs was to devise a method of problem analysis targeted on particular issues and specific, situationally relevant prophylactic measures. It diagnosed the problem thus:

> In the development of broader crime prevention measures what has tended to be lacking has been the coherent and systematic marshalling of . . . information in respect of the circumstances surrounding particular types of offence.

and its solution as follows:

> An examination of the situation in which a particular type of offence takes place can reveal the conditions necessary for or conducive to its commission and can suggest preventive measures which relate directly to these conditions (para. 12).

The Working Group termed this approach situational prevention. In principle, situational prevention favours neither physical nor social measures because:

> crime results from the interplay of circumstantial and motivational factors and the balance of the two varies with different crimes. The development of any effective measures depends on considering this balance in relation to specific crimes and on assessing the practicability of different kinds of intervention, which may draw on either [social] or [physical], measures (para. 11).

The Working Group emphasised that situational prevention was not to be regarded as a method of prevention *per se* and certainly not as a cure-all:

> The situational approach should not be seen as providing new and certain answers on how to prevent crime or necessarily as supplying any fresh individual techniques. Rather it is intended to make up for the limited ability of the traditional approaches to meet the need for a broader based crime prevention initiative. It would facilitate the more systematic and coherent application of existing techniques, and would provide the framework in which present knowledge could be exploited and empirically tested, and the foundation on which new knowledge may be built up (para. 21).

The approach would involve

a. basic crimes analysis (using information held by all relevant agencies) which could be used to identify further research requirements and to identify possible lines of action;
b. the testing of recommended action in experimental trials and in particular its cost effectiveness; and
c. the identification of areas where interdepartmental consultation and cooperation looks to be a necessary precondition of effective prevention.

As a result of the Working Group's recommendations the Home Office set up a 'demonstration project' aimed at testing the application of the situational approach to reducing vandalism in schools. The disappointing results of this project are discussed in the following chapter.

Subsequent developments

Despite the Working Group's sceptical view of the existing basis for a Home Office crime prevention initiative aimed at involving other agencies and government departments, and despite the subsequent fate of its situational demonstration project, the Home Office has continued to affirm a faith in the potential effectiveness of crime prevention if only the right seams of collective endeavour can be identified and mined. In 1982 it initiated discussions between top officials from seven other government departments which it thought had (or should have) an interest in preventing crime. This group began from the premiss that neither central government departments nor local services were as crime conscious as they might be and it endorsed the value of developing the situational approach to prevention. But whereas the 1976 Working Group had specifically held back from championing the situational approach as an *answer* to crime and had preferred to see it as an approach whose efficacy needed to be tested, the interdepartmental group entertained no such doubts. Situational prevention, it felt, offered 'the best immediate prospect for specific crime reduction' (Home Office, 1983d, para. 4).

The group concluded first, that the preventive element in all police work, not just the specialist crime prevention service, should be developed and expanded; second, that this work should include other local agencies; and third, in marked contrast to the Ditchley circular, that rather than wait for the police to take the lead, these other agencies should set up suitable administrative arrangements by which to secure greater collaboration. These policy prescriptions were reiterated in a subsequent interdepartmental seminar hosted by the Home Office and designed to bolster and disseminate the value of the 'coordinated approach' (Home Office, 1983e); in a circular on crime prevention issued jointly by the departments that were party to these discussions; and in the setting up of a new Crime Prevention Unit based at the Home Office. The circular (which like the Ditchley circular, has been widely circulated outside the police service) begins with the conventional and by now familiar policy wisdom that preventing crime is a task for the whole community. It goes on to commend its recipients to adopt both a coordinated and a situational approach to prevention. Here the key steps are collation and analysis of relevant information; devising situationally specific solutions; the setting up of appropriate liaison machinery to plan and implement crime prevention measures; and an emphasis on experiment and monitoring.

This approach to prevention also forms the basis of the terms of reference of the Crime Prevention Unit. With a mix of research and administrative staff, its job is to work with local agencies to set up research and development projects and to help them design, implement and evaluate their own initiatives. Like the Home Office Standing Committee on Crime Prevention, an important function of the Crime Prevention Unit is declaratory. At the same time as providing a source of practical help to them, it provides a channel for propagandising the message that crime prevention is important to the constituencies that the government wants to reach.

Crimes analysis: situatiuonal crime prevention revisited

On the Home Office model, the basis of both situational crime prevention and coordinated, collaborative effort is crimes analysis. Crimes analysis is based on the premiss that before sensible crime prevention strategies can be devised, people need to know where and when particular crimes occur, why they occur, how they occur and who commits them. This sounds fair enough. However, the actual usefulness of crimes analysis as a way of creating a sounder intellectual and practical base for preventive effort is itself based on a number of assumptions, each of which can be questioned. They are:

that crime follows patterns, such that it is possible not only to discern but also to predict when and where concentrations of particular crimes occur;

that sensible policy prescription will follow on fairly naturally from knowledge of how crime is patterned; and

that the police are both willing and able to undertake the kinds of analysis required, not just as a one-off, but as a way of thinking about and organising strategies of prevention.

Despite the potentially very large amount of information that police forces can collect about crime, very little of it has been put to detailed analytical use and virtually none of it has been made available publicly as a basis for discussion about what ought to be done.[15] Instead it is necessary to turn to other sources for information about the temporal and spatial distribution of crime. As part of its programme of research designed to put situational analysis more firmly on the map, the Home Office has recently funded or carried out four studies which use crimes analysis as a basis for trying to devise preventive strategies. These are:

three studies of violent incidents in city centres (Ramsay, 1982, Poyner, 1981 and Hope, 1985, Ch. 4), and a study of school burglaries (Hope, 1982 and 1985, Ch. 2).

The findings of these studies differ according to the type of crime examined but some general lessons can be drawn from them. They confirm that crime follows patterns and that it is possible to specify locations or times of day where people and/or property are more at risk than at others. In Hope's study, for example, three-quarters of burglaries occurred in one-third of the schools he studied. In Ramsay's study, two-thirds of 'violent and disruptive' incidents in a city centre either occurred in, or were linked to, pubs and clubs. Poyner found that two-thirds of assaults in public places were linked to specific locations and times, such as bus stops in the rush hour, markets and pedestrian subways.

So far so good. However although each of the above studies found that crimes were patterned, they were still rare events, even in relatively high-risk locations. Poyner, for example, identifies markets as being places where certain sorts of crimes (thefts from shopping bags) were concentrated. Yet even here, the number of thefts amounted to only one per week per market. In both Hope's view and Ramsay's view, the rarity of crime either considerably limits the scope for crime prevention interventions or it means that preventive measures are unlikely to be cost effective. It is clear therefore that crimes analysis does not necessarily yield useful information about crime in the sense of suggesting prescriptions for action.

There are other drawbacks to crimes analysis. For one thing it is costly. Poyner's study for example, cost £25,000. The Home Office Working Group on Crime Prevention thought that the analytical work involved in situational crimes analysis would be 'substantial'. This is of some importance since the government has made it clear that no new money will be available for preventive initiatives. A significant shift in force priorities will, therefore, be necessary to free resources from other activities if crimes analysis is to take hold.

Perhaps the greater difficulty is that forces are not at present equipped to carry it out. Crime prevention departments in particular lack the expertise and have in the past set little store by the analytical method and have given low priority to analytical thinking. This is not to say, of course, that they should not in future begin to develop the necessary expertise. Even simple analyses may teach the police facts about the distribution of crime of which they have hitherto been unaware and help in the business of designing preventive strategies. Although success in preventing crime is by no means guaranteed by this method, detailed and systematic knowledge cannot but provide a sounder and more consistent basis for action than the patchy information presently used. As it is, the lack of detailed analytical information frequently makes it difficult to determine whether crime prevention schemes are worth embarking upon and whether or not they have been successful. By the same token clear and unambiguous information can not only reveal the failure of individual initiatives but more fundamentally can call into question the policy on which the initiatives are based. The idea that the 'community' holds solutions to the problems of preventing crime is one such policy. In the next chapter I examine more closely some of the evidence for this proposition.

Notes

1. For example, the Greater London Council, in response to the draft Home Office circular on crime prevention issued in 1983, declares the circular's opening statement — that the police alone cannot prevent crime and the involvement of other agencies is needed to create an effective crime prevention strategy — to be a 'redefinition' of crime prevention. It is, moreover, a redefinition which has 'occurred swiftly' (Greater London Council, 1983a). Similar views can be found in the police service. In a review of neighbourhood watch schemes, the head of the crime prevention department in the Metropolitan Police has written 'only in the last two years have we seen any constructive moves to restore the primacy of crime prevention through policies to encourage police to work with the community to reduce crime' (Turner, 1984, p. 1).

2. Represented on the Standing Committee are: the Home Office (which chairs it), the Scottish Home and Health Department, the CBI, the National Chamber of Trade, the Association for Prevention of Theft in Shops, the British Insurance Association, the Committee of Lloyds, the Committee of London Clearing Banks, the Association of British Chambers of Commerce, the British Security Industry Association, the TUC, ACPO, the Metropolitan Police, and the International Professional Security Association. In 1983, the Standing Committee's membership was extended to include representatives from other central government departments and from local government: the Department of the Environment, Department of Health and Social Security, Department of Education, Association of Metropolitan Authorities, Association of County Councils and Association of District Councils. In addition, the chairmanship of the Committee was upgraded from official to ministerial level.

3. It is revealing that in the Policy Studies Institute study of the Metropolitan Police (Smith, 1983, vol. III), where police officers were asked, for each of ten specialisms, a series of questions aimed at tapping their own experience and aspirations, crime prevention was not thought to be important enough even to be included in the list.

4. Except in the Metropolitan Police, where the head of the crime prevention department is a superintendent, and the Crime Prevention Centre, which is headed by a chief superintendent. John Wheeler MP, in a recent pamphlet on crime prevention and the police, recommends that the crime prevention service 'should be strengthened by the injection of vigorous seniors'! (Wheeler, 1980, p. 21).

5. A report on the Home Office Crime Prevention Centre, issued in 1979, noted that some forces nominated officers for standard courses for what appeared to be 'post service' training. At one stage, about one-third of the students were over 45 or had completed

25 years' service (Association of Chief Police Officers, 1979, para. 10.1). In a more recent survey in one Area of the Metropolitan Police District, the average length of service of sixteen crime prevention officers and their deputies on appointment was 18 years (Metropolitan Police, 1984, paras. 15.1 and 15.2). The Metropolitan Police requires officers to have at least 10 years' service before they become eligible for appointment as a crime prevention officer.

6. For example, the assumption that 1½ hours are needed to carry out and write up a standard domestic security survey, the ratio of one crime prevention officer to every 30,000 households means that it would take over 30 years for the available officers to survey each household, even if they were to do nothing else. Winchester and Jackson note that because of other demands on crime prevention officers' time, fewer than 0.5 per cent of the households in one sub-division in Kent that they researched received a crime prevention survey in any one year (Winchester and Jackson, 1982, p. 11). On this basis and with current manpower, it would take 200 years before every household would receive a survey.

7. The bread and butter of the Crime Prevention Centre's work is the provision of four-week basic training courses for newly appointed crime prevention officers. The Centre runs seven or eight of these each year. It also runs week-long refresher courses for crime prevention officers with at least three years' service (three a year); an annual seminar for heads of crime prevention departments; an annual, week-long course for burglary insurance surveyors; and a one-week course for Home Office drugs inspectors.

8. These were: communicating crime prevention; defensible space and architect liaison; community involvement and the role of crime prevention panels; victim support; and vandalism liaison projects.

9. *Designing out crime* includes studies of vandalism and car theft. Subsequent research published as part of the Unit's crime prevention programme includes a study of burglary in schools (Hope, 1982 and 1985, Ch. 2); of crime in a city centre (Ramsay, 1982 and Hope, 1985, Ch. 4); and two studies of residential burglary (Winchester and Jackson, 1982; Maguire and Bennett, 1982). This last study, though not carried out by the Home Office, was funded by it.

10. Partial security was defined as 'some doors without mortice deadlock/doublelock, and/or some downstairs windows without window locks'; and poor security as 'no mortice deadlocks/double locks and no window locks' (Winchester and Jackson, 1982, Table 3.2).

11. So far as I know neither campaign has been evaluated in the sense of testing whether it made people more aware of the risks of crime and more prone to take precautions. In the case of the Lambeth initiative, recorded street crime (that is robberies and thefts from the person) fell following the publicity campaign. The reasons for this reduction are difficult to disentangle, since the publicity drive was only one of several policing initiatives in the area at the time. Others included increased consultation with the community over policing operations, more foot patrols and greater targetting and surveillance of possible suspects. In addition, the advice was not specifically aimed at local women, nor at high-risk groups (if such existed) among them. It took the form of a pamphlet called *Woman Alone*, published by a life-assurance company and aimed at women in general.

12. The British Crime Survey calculated the risk of the 'statistically average' person becoming a victim as follows:

a robbery every five centuries
an assault resulting in injury (even if slight) once every century
a family car stolen or taken by joy-riders once every 60 years
a burglary in the home once every 40 years (Hough and Mayhew, 1983, p. 15).

13. To fit mortice deadlocks to front and back doors and downstairs window locks to the average three-bedroomed house (i.e. the minimum level of security likely to be recommended by a crime prevention officer) would cost between £50 and £100 (the lower figure

is for a do-it-yourself installation). The cost of installing a burglar alarm in a similar property is upwards of £300, added to which is an annual maintenance charge of around 10 per cent of the cost of installation.

14. The Working Group's report was not published. Its approach to its work and its recommendations are described in Gladstone, 1980, Ch. 3.

15. One exception is the geographical spot-mapping exercises carried out by Devon and Cornwall Constabulary and described in Chapter 5. Many forces also make available information on highly localised crime patterns to crime prevention panels, neighbourhood watch schemes and consultative committees and this seems to be a growing trend. So far as I know, however, as a form of public education, the kind of analysis and method of presentation employed in Devon and Cornwall was, if not unique, then certainly very uncommon.

5 CRIME PREVENTION IN PRACTICE

In this chapter I shall try to illustrate some of the main theoretical and practical issues which were raised in the last one, by describing examples of crime prevention projects in action. As I have explained, one of the main aims of recent government initiatives is to generate more crime prevention activity in forces and to encourage the growth of good practice based on careful monitoring of the results of those initiatives. Yet in the past, forces have not been much inclined to experiment with different crime prevention methods and approaches, nor have they been geared to collecting and analysing information about them. Hence the relatively small number of initiatives described here.[1]

The paucity of material on force initiatives obviously limits the lessons that can be drawn from them. So does the (often partial) way in which evidence about them has been collected and reviewed. In five of the seven initiatives reviewed below, police accounts are the only or main source of information about them. The police clearly have an interest in presenting their activity in the best possible light and they have tended to do so. I shall comment on the nature and quality of the evidence about the effects and effectiveness of each initiative as I deal with it. Each of them has attracted the label 'community crime prevention' but the range of ideas they embody is wide. It covers direct appeals to individual self interest; the creation of forums in which crime prevention ideas can be discussed and action taken; and attempts to create a sense of common purpose and mutual self help and/or to improve the quality of life in specific neighbourhoods. The first two initiatives (in Northumbria) are concerned solely with physical prevention. They raise questions of how and why defensive measures fail and how even simple prescriptions can come unstuck in the process of implementing them. The third initiative (in Humberside) was devised as a response to the Ditchley circular (see page 58). It raises questions of how and on what criteria such initiatives are to be judged and who is best placed to collect the information on which such judgements can be made, and how schemes come to stand as exemplars of successful practice. The fourth initiative (from South Wales) again raises questions about how effectiveness should be judged. The fifth and sixth examples (a project from Devon and Cornwall, and the Home Office demonstration project in Greater Manchester) have been chosen because of the issues they raise about the appropriateness and

68

effectiveness of cooperative strategies as answers to crime prevention problems. The final initiative (neighbourhood watch, which is not specific to any force) is used to explore some of the factors affecting the willingness and ability of ordinary people to become involved in organised crime prevention activity.[2]

Two security projects: Felling and Scotswood

In 1979, Northumbria Police received funds from the Inner City Partnership scheme to provide basic security fitments to every dwelling on two local authority housing estates. Both estates were thought to suffer from burglary and on neither were the existing standards of security very good. It was hypothesised that the improved security would reduce the incidence of burglary and help residents feel safer. The Felling scheme was monitored by the police (Northumbria Police, undated) and the Scotswood scheme by Newcastle-upon-Tyne Polytechnic (Allatt, 1984a and b).

Scotswood

The security in an entire area of nearly 800 dwellings was upgraded — at an average cost of £34 per dwelling — by fitting deadlocks to front and back doors, door safety chains where appropriate and locks to all ground floor windows. Recorded burglary statistics were monitored for this target estate, for a control area and for two likely displacement areas. In addition, interviews were sought with one member from each of one-half of the households in both the target and control areas, before and after the new security measures were installed. The interviews concentrated on changes in anxiety levels, discrepancies between the number of burglaries reported by tenants in the interviews and those in police records and the apparent effectiveness or ineffectiveness of the security devices in cases of successful and unsuccessful burglary.

Incidence of burglary. High reporting rates for burglary meant that burglaries recorded by the police could be used as an accurate substitute measure for the number of burglaries committed (Allatt, 1984a, p. 105). Police figures showed that for the year following the installation of the new locks, burglaries on the target estate remained high but steady, while those on the control estate and the two displacement estates almost doubled. This pattern of disparity continued over a subsequent year, suggesting that the improved security helped to deter potential burglars, but perhaps at the cost of sending them elsewhere. Successfully deterred burglars seem also to have turned to other crimes. Thefts, robberies and burglaries to premises other than dwellings increased much more markedly in Scotswood than on the control estate. Allatt concludes, however, that the amount of crime thus displaced was less than the number of burglaries prevented through better security. The project thus seems to have provided overall gains for Scotswood residents in terms of the numbers of crimes committed in their community.

The use and effectiveness of security devices. Whether potential burglars were being realistic in feeling deterred is another matter. Twenty-four of the 205 residents interviewed reported having been burgled on at least one occasion after locks had been fitted. In ten of these cases, locks had not been in use at the point where the burglar entered but in only a minority did this result from householders' negligence. The main reasons for failure of security were that locks had not been fitted properly, or at all, or had broken and had not been replaced by the works department. Allatt points up the implications for installation and maintenance policies of findings such as these and she suggests that with the passing of time, security installation programmes may well lose their initial effectiveness.

Residents' anxieties. An unusual feature of the Scotswood project was that attempts were made not only to assess the effects on levels of crime but also on residents' feelings of safety.

The majority of Scotswood residents (80 per cent) and residents on the control estate (58 per cent) reported that 'quite a lot' or 'a great deal' of crime occurred on the estate where they lived. The incidence of burglary dominated these perceptions. Installation of locks did little to affect these perceptions in Scotswood. What did seem to be affected however was people's assessments of the likelihood of becoming a victim. Significantly fewer of those interviewed in Scotswood after locks had been installed expressed worries of this kind than had done so before the security installations: 40 per cent as against 53 per cent. (This contrasted with the control estate, where initial levels of worry were similar to those in Scotswood but where there was a small increase in the proportion of residents who said that they worried about the prospect of being burgled.) In addition to this measure of increased security, a majority of residents felt that the security hardware had helped to prevent burglary, and some of them (about a quarter) said that it made them feel safer.

Felling

The Felling project was in many respects similar to the one in Scotswood. About 200 houses (the 'target estate') were fitted with locks to all ground floor windows and doors. The doors, which were flimsily built, were reinforced with plywood in most of the houses and a safety chain was fitted to the front door. The total cost was just over £10,000 — about £50 per dwelling.

The effect of the scheme was assessed by comparing recorded burglary and attempted burglary figures for the three years before security was upgraded with figures for the two years afterwards. (The police felt that most burglary was reported to them so that recorded crime would accurately reflect actual levels of crime.) Similar statistics were collected for a nearby control area and also for a wider area around the target estate in order to test for possible displacement of burglary elsewhere. A small sample of residents (just over 30) were asked what they thought of the security devices and, if they had been burgled, how the burglar had got into the house.

The upgraded security appears to have had no effect on the number of burglaries recorded for the target estate, the control area or the displacement area. There were a number of reasons for this. First, the number of recorded burglaries in each of the three areas and for each of the three years prior to the locks being fitted was so small that very marked changes in the incidence of the crime would have had to occur before reliable trends were discernible. (For example, the incidence of burglary on the target estate was around 10 per year.) Secondly, the way in which the security fittings were designed and installed left a great deal to be desired and illustrates how easily even straightforward initiatives can go awry through lack of care and foresight. One key opened all the window locks on the estate and four burglaries in the two years following the installation of the locks (almost a quarter of the total) occurred when the burglar was able to unlock a window with a duplicate key (possibly his own), after breaking a pane of glass. The front door locks posed another problem. When they were fitted, the original locks were not removed and to open the door two keys had to be inserted and turned simultaneously. Both hands were needed to do this. As a result 'nearly all' of the surveyed households left the new front door lock permanently on the latch, thus entirely negating the point of fitting it in the first place.

The Felling project was aimed not only at reducing the incidence of burglary on the estate but also at making people living there feel safer. The police evaluation of the scheme provides virtually no evidence on this point. It does, however, conclude: 'Since the title of the project was

''The Prevention of Fear'', there is every reason to suppose that fear was reduced.'

Community campaigning and casework: the Grange Project

The Grange Project was set up by the Humberside Police in 1979 in response to the Ditchley circular which urged a coordinated approach to juvenile delinquency. It was planned as a multi-agency approach to the problems of juvenile crime on two local authority estates in Grimsby. It involved the local police, who instigated the project, education and housing departments and the probation and social services. The Humberside Police described its objectives as follows:

To develop co-operation between the police and other services responsible for dealing with juveniles, in activities which might help to prevent anti-social behaviour.

To establish a central clearing house, between each of the agencies involved, for the collation and dissemination of views and information which would assist in helping children at risk.

To regard the experiment as a pilot scheme and consider the effects with a view to future implementation in other suitable locations within the Humberside Police area.

To monitor the activities undertaken on the experimental area as an on-going project, hence keeping the activities and their effects under review, and presenting this information to the Chief Constable.

For members of the police juvenile liaison department to consult with the various tenants' organisations and parent/teacher associations or with any organisation within either the public or private sector which may be in a position to make a meaningful contribution.

To increase the awareness of juveniles of their responsibilities towards the society in which they live.

By involvement with the residents of the experimental area, to create a better community spirit.

To reduce the involvement of juveniles in anti-social behaviour.

To reduce the number of offences committed by juveniles resident on the experimental area.

To reduce the rate at which children at risk of becoming offenders appear in the official statistics as actual offenders.

To influence juveniles who come to the notice of the police as offenders for the first time, so that they do not re-offend (Humberside Police, undated, pp. 3–5).

The scheme was monitored over the first year of its existence by the Humberside Police (Humberside Police, 1981).

The Grange Project combined two principal ideas about the origins of juvenile crime and how to tackle it. First, it was a hearts and minds campaign, with a strong emphasis on improving the behaviour of young people, particularly through family casework and through educational programmes. Police community liaison officers visited the homes of all children coming to police notice. Their job was to 'counsel families, including other children in the family, with a primary object of preventing any further similar behaviour' (Humberside Police, undated, pp. 6–7). In addition, a schools liaison programme was introduced into all schools on the estates, with particular attention being paid to 9–11 year olds. A second strand of the project was the encouragement of community activities and a less crime-prone environment. Two residents' associations were formed which lobbied the local council for environmental improvements, and undertook self-help work. The Project Consultative Group launched an appeal for funds for a children's playground. Two community centres were set up, which not only served as bases for the residents' associations but also as 'surgeries' for the police, social services, housing department and local councillors. The estate was already served by resident beat officers. As the project became established, they were encouraged to become increasingly involved in planning and committee work.

The Grange Project was evaluated by the Humberside Police using statistics of juveniles from the estate coming to police notice. The residents' associations, local constables, director of housing, divisional education officer and assistant chief probation officer were all canvassed for their views on the state of cooperation between police and local services; how aware juveniles were of their social responsibilities and how involved in anti-social behaviour; and the strength of community spirit.

The Grange Project has been widely advertised as a success (see successive annual reports of the chief constable, Home Office, 1983d, pp. 3 and 49, and Parliamentary All-Party Penal Affairs Group, pp. 97–8).[3] It is, however, difficult for an outsider to assess the extent to which this verdict is warranted. From their reported comments, it is clear that most of those closely involved in running the project[4] were strongly committed to it, were enthusiastic about its aims, welcomed the opportunity to work with other agencies to tackle common problems and believed that the project had been and would continue to be a success. In addition, and at the more practical level of getting things done, the project was clearly successful in spawning a number of valued initiatives, such as the two local residents' associations. Several respondents felt that such initiatives were in themselves evidence of the greater community spirit and cooperation that the scheme was designed to foster. Such comments of course run the risk of generalising from respondents' own experiences and the Grange Project evaluation was not designed to test the extent to which a more representative sample of residents felt that they too had benefited from what was being done in their name; nor did it seek the views of the project fieldworkers. It is also important to remember that the main rationale for the scheme was to reduce juvenile crime and induce a greater sense of social responsibility among young people. Here the evidence of success is equivocal. Although several respondents saw evidence of a reduction in criminal and anti-social behaviour among the young people for whom they had professional responsibilities, others felt it would take several years before any improvements would show themselves. This last point — that the project initiatives could only be expected to make an impact on behaviour in the longer term — is repeatedly emphasised in the Humberside Police evaluation of the scheme. That said, the recorded crime figures and the figures of juveniles coming to the notice of the police during the first year of the project fail to support other, more optimistic claims for the initial success of the scheme. The number of juveniles coming to notice rose in line with the trend established over the previous five years (Humberside Police, undated, para. 1.2.6). The total amount of recorded crime on the estate also rose.

Individual entrepreneurship: crime prevention in Merthyr Tydfil

South Wales Constabulary has been very active in the field of community crime prevention, often through the efforts of a few pioneering and entrepreneurial individuals. In 1979 Merthyr Tydfil was chosen for the launch of a two-man anti-vandal team, whose main function was to reduce the high level of vandalism in the town. The scheme was highly publicised in the local press and is fully described in Hall (1981). Hall studied the scheme by accompanying the two officers on patrol and by talking to their colleagues and supervisors. He also talked to key members of local organisations, to local children and to victims of vandalism.

The two officers who formed the anti-vandal team had been given a brief to 'do something' about vandalism. What to do was left up to them. The main method they chose was informal reparation. Using local contacts and local knowledge, they identified who was responsible for causing the damage, most of it graffiti. Offenders, with their parents, attended the police station and were asked to make good the damage they had caused. They were told that failure to do so would make them liable to prosecution. No records were kept of this unofficial action nor of the amount of damage made good as a result of it but Hall notes that during the first 21 months of the scheme, the two officers made 117 arrests and detected those responsible for causing £110,000 worth of criminal damage.

Because so little information was available to him on the incidence and distribution of vandalism in Merthyr, Hall's account of the two officers' work concentrates less on its practical outcomes than on how the officers were seen by and related to the wider community. He claims widespread support for the officers' initiatives not only amongst local people but also by the offenders themselves. He argues that the officers' work not only had a restorative function but a preventive one too and that their use of informal methods encouraged people to give more information to the police and thus prevent and detect more crime. In addition Hall argues that the policing approach and style they adopted enabled the officers to activate sources of community activity and goodwill that might otherwise have lain dormant. To illustrate this, he describes how a vandalised building was repaired by those who had damaged it, who later proposed that it be used as a community meeting place and helped to raise funds for converting and renovating it.

Hall's claims for the Merthyr scheme are far-reaching: that it reduced vandalism, promoted community solidarity and improved police-community relationships (particularly police-youth relationships), improvements which themselves led to less crime and to improved methods of detecting it. By no means all of these claims can be substantiated on the basis of the information which Hall collected: for example, he was unable to document the extent of vandalism in Merthyr, or to say much about people's perceptions of it; and he spoke to only a limited number of local residents in coming to his conclusions. None the less his account raises interesting issues of how particular policing styles, characterised in this instance by informal contact and a willingness to take informal action, can help to prevent crime. If the work of beat officers is to become more explicitly prevention-oriented, more accurate, unvarnished accounts of the day-to-day work of individual patrol officers would be helpful.[5] So would some way of relating that work more systematically to tests of achievement.

Coordinated crime prevention in action: Devon and Cornwall and the Home Office situational demonstration project

The idea that cooperative effort and/or coordination promise a way forward for preventive policies underlies each of the initiatives described above. Research is, however, beginning to suggest that, far from being a panacea, coordination is not only difficult to achieve but may even hinder effective action. This is the main message that emerges from the Home Office account of its situational demonstration project and it is foreshadowed in the various accounts of the work of Devon and Cornwall Constabulary's Crime Prevention Support Unit. For the most part, however, the potential problems of coordination are largely unmentioned in official policy pronouncements or in police accounts of their own initiatives.[6] This is hardly surprising given the appeal of coordination as a way out of what might otherwise be a policy impasse, that is, the apparent failure of the institution charged with preventing crime — the police — to make the desired impact. In such circumstances, the appeal of coordination lies in its recognition of the complexities of the situations in which crimes occur and in its promise that they can be dealt with in a programme of action where the partial knowledge of interested parties can be pooled and their fragmented responsibilities reconciled. Thus there is now an official recognition that the activities of many different institutions create conditions in which crime becomes more or less likely, and a greater ability to specify what those conditions are. There has also been a greater determination to call those institutions to account for their failure to take crime prevention seriously and a greater willingness to do so. Coordinated crime prevention has come to epitomise *par excellence* the belief that policing problems can be solved if a consensus can be reached by appropriate agencies about how to proceed.

Coordinated crime prevention in Devon and Cornwall

The work of Devon and Cornwall Constabulary's Crime Prevention Support Unit and its offshoot, the Exeter Community Policing Consultative Group, is probably one of the earliest attempts to generate a coordinated, multi-agency approach to prevention. The Unit was established to give practical effect to John Alderson's ideas that the police should seek to 'motivate the good' in society and stimulate informal community control. Its work has been documented by the superintendent in charge of it (Moore, 1978; Moore and Brown, 1981) and by the National Association for the Care and Resettlement of Offenders (NACRO), which was invited to study it (Blaber, 1979).

CPSU's terms of reference were:

> to examine facts and statistics in selected police areas with a view to the identification of crime and community problems;
> to produce and experiment with new ideas in crime prevention initiatives;
> to encourage and direct available police resources to the prevention of crime; and
> to harness available public support in activities to teach good citizenship and thereby prevent crime (quoted in Blaber, p. 10).

An important innovatory feature of CPSU was its use of crimes analysis as a starting point for thinking about how to proceed. It began with analyses of juvenile crime — spot-maps showing when and where such crime was committed and how it was distributed in relation to features of the environment such as public transport routes, pubs and schools. CPSU deliberately disseminated this information as widely as possible, on the assumption that the more information people were given about crime, the more likely they were to want to take action against it. The maps were also used to propagate the message that crime arose from certain features of community life and could therefore best be tackled in and with the community.

From this starting point two main strategies evolved. One involved the police working directly with local residents in various crime prevention and community involvement activities. The most important of these were play and recreational schemes, organised by the police for young people in school holidays, and the setting up of a community association on a local authority housing estate. CPSU's other main strategy was to create a forum for improving cooperation and coordination between the police and local authority agencies. This forum was the Exeter Community Policing Consultative Group. It had as its terms of reference:

> to provide a forum for considering ways to reduce crime by social as well as police action and for sharing respective problems and initiatives;

to identify community needs, and to formulate possible action through a multi-discipline approach and to report where necessary to appropriate bodies;
to maximise the use of available resources;
to review, support and monitor local community initiatives; and
to determine and promote training for a programme of multi-disciplinary approach (Moore and Brown, 1981, p. 53).

The group contained representatives from the local authority, transport, education and highways departments, district and county councillors, the local press, churches, and trade unions and magistracy and from the Department of Health and Social Security and the Department of Employment. Moore and Brown describe the group's 'peak achievements' as the creation of a joint agency training programme and the development of a 'more general advisory role', which included advising on local authority planning applications (ibid., p. 59).

CPSU's work has never been fully evaluated but from the available descriptions of it two sets of interesting points emerge. The first set relates to the relationship CPSU sought to establish with other agencies and the resistances it met to doing this. The second set has to do with CPSU's effects on the problems it set out to tackle — crime, especially juvenile crime — and the attitude it came to adopt to the feasibility and relevance of pursuing such a goal.

Moore and Brown's book is a refreshingly warts-and-all account of the difficulties in getting coordinated initiatives off the ground. In its early days, the Exeter Policing Consultative Group floundered along without any clear idea of where it was going or how to get there and it proved difficult to create a sense of common purpose amongst its members. Part of this trouble was administrative. Although the police were nominally in charge of the group, they lacked experience in servicing a committee and of communicating with local authority departments and they had little knowledge of the local government machine. These deficiencies were serious enough not just to reduce the practical impact that the group had,[7] they also threatened its existence. Most of these difficulties seem eventually to have been overcome, but other, more fundamental problems remained: in particular, suspicion and reserve towards the police on the part of other agencies and an ambivalence about their role. This ambivalence surfaced in a number of ways. Agencies were suspicious of police attempts to get them to share data and a police-initiated play scheme ran into difficulties with other agencies and with local residents, who mistrusted police motives for setting it up. Other conflicts arose (though Moore and Brown give no details of these) when the various parties to the enterprise lacked a common starting point, philosophy and language for talking about what were supposed to be common problems. In this sense, the group seems to have heightened the sense that agencies were working at cross-purposes rather than dissipating it. As a result, a number of joint training initiatives were set up which were aimed at helping agencies understand and appreciate others' perspectives on problems.

The effects of CPSU initiatives on the problems it set out to solve are difficult to discern, partly because of the ambivalence which was felt about the police role among those with whom it wished to work, partly because of what seems to have been an eventual retreat from the objective of preventing crime. Within the Exeter Policing Consultative Group, this ambivalence was at least partly resolved in a broader remit for the group giving less prominence to the police role (there were pressures to have the word 'policing' dropped from the group's title) and putting more emphasis on the delivery of non-police services to the community. For its part, CPSU seems to have in effect abandoned the idea that it was primarily in the business of preventing crime as it became progressively more enthused with the idea of doing community work: the play-schemes were the most obvious evidence of this. In their account, Moore and Brown periodically flirt with the notion that crime was prevented by CPSU's activities, only to draw away from the full implications of accepting that this might be the ultimate test of the Unit's effectiveness. Despite the importance it attached to crimes analysis as a way of goading people into action, CPSU seem to have found little incentive to monitor crime figures and use them to evaluate its own initiatives. The 'community hypothesis', that is, that communities can be motivated to regulate themselves once stimulated to do so by appropriate leadership, thus remains largely untested by the CPSU experiment. Instead, CPSU chose to present the value and importance of its work in quite other ways: by reference to its enthusiasm, crusading spirit, vigour and initiative, and its preparedness to learn from other points of view. It is ultimately on these qualities that we are invited to judge its worth.

Coordinated crime prevention in Greater Manchester

The problems of ensuring purposeful and effective cooperative working are a recurring theme in the accounts of the Home Office situational demonstration project. Here the aims were fourfold:

to assist the Home Office in broadening the focus of its work on crime prevention, so that it can develop the means for providing wider assistance to other departments and agencies, both nationally and locally, on the crime prevention aspects of their policies;·
to test the recommended new approach to crime prevention, in relation to the practicability of applying it to a specific crime and to its effectiveness in identifying viable crime prevention measures;
to evaluate specific measures for reducing the incidence of vandalism in schools; and
to facilitate improved cooperation on crime prevention between local authorities, the police and other local agencies; and, in particular, to involve school authorities in tackling the problem of vandalism (Gladstone, 1980, p. 71).

Three agencies were involved in the initial stages of the project: the Greater Manchester Police, Manchester City Education Department, and the Home Office, which provided expert crime prevention advice through its Crime Prevention Centre, funded a part-time project coordinator and provided research backing. The project was focused on eleven schools. A 'diagnostic package' was prepared for each one. This consisted of a schedule for collecting information from heads of schools and from a crime prevention survey about the types of damage the school suffered, when and where the damage occurred and the kinds of precautions that were taken against it. The aim of this was 'to supply a procedure which would guide the user from a precise definition of those problems, to appropriate recommendations for action' (ibid., p. 22). Relevant information was also sought from the city planning department, which provided information about existing and planned leisure provision in the areas surrounding each school. Using the information in the diagnostic package, representatives from each school, and from the education, direct works, social services and planning departments produced agreed recommendations about what needed to be done.

The project was evaluated using records of requests to repair damage (whether accidental or deliberate) to the physical fabric of schools. The process of implementing the recommendations was also carefully monitored.

The situational demonstration project was not a success. After two years, the incidence of damage to schools remained unaffected. Relatively few of the recommended crime prevention measures had been put into effect. After a year, only five out of a total of 30 recommendations had been implemented; after two years, only half of them had. At only two

Crime Prevention in Practice 81

schools was the full package of recommendations implemented; and at three schools, no recommendation was implemented (Hope and Murphy, 1983, p. 41).

Although it would be difficult to regard the situational demonstration project as a good advertisement for the merits of coordinated crime prevention, its failure to deliver the goods was not for want of effort. The method of problem analysis it used was careful and thorough and the diagnostic package that was devised for schools deserves to have been more widely disseminated and used. Much effort was put into devising an information base for long-term monitoring and evaluation. Considerable effort and resources (much more than would be normal or even practicable for a force crime prevention department to supply) went into servicing the consultative machinery that formed the basis of the co-ordinated approach. The project was special — a 'demonstration' of what could be achieved — and central government was committed to evaluating it. Thus there was a far greater incentive to deliver results than is the case with most crime prevention efforts. Finally, most of the measures chosen for implementation, like applying anti-climb paint to drainpipes and fitting toughened glass in windows, seemed to be straightforward and non-controversial and the locus of responsibility for implementing them was clear and unambiguous. In other words, as an exercise in rational planning, the project seemed to have everything going for it. Why then did it fail?

In their review of the history of the project, Hope and Murphy argue that it failed because it was based on a set of wrong assumptions about how recommendations would be translated into action. The project largely took for granted the process of implementation. A rational solution to the problem of vandalism in schools had been devised; the rational response was to implement it. In practice, those responsible for implementing the recommendations were frequently reluctant or unable to do so. Some of the difficulties they faced were technical and could probably have been overcome given time, effort and money, even though in practice these commodities were in short supply. Other difficulties were more fundamental. They arose from the fact that those responsible for ensuring the work was done were already fully occupied or had other more pressing interests or constituencies to satisfy and were unwilling or unable to give priority to crime prevention.

While it is clearly tempting to recommend even greater communication and liaison between the parties to a coordinated approach as a solution to problems such as these, Hope and Murphy's analysis suggests that in many respects it would be futile to do so. Ensuring greater communication and creating a common approach to a problem not only has resource costs, it also assumes an agreement about priorities which is often unlikely to obtain in practice. What may be an important consideration of policy from the viewpoint of one institution may be of minor importance or even irrelevant from the viewpoint of another. No amount of resort to models of rational decision-making or appeals to the virtue of collaborative effort can obscure the fact that the practice of coordinated crime prevention reveals as many impediments to the implementation of change as it is designed to remove. If there is any lesson to be drawn from the situational demonstration project and the Devon and Cornwall crime prevention initiatives, it is not that coordinated crime prevention prevents crime. It is rather that it entails a highly problematic set of prescriptions whose outcomes are unpredictable. In this, coordinated crime prevention is no different from any other crime prevention approach.

Looking and listening: neighbourhood watch

Neighbourhood watch is being vigorously promoted as a highly promising way of reducing crime. It is an American import, but with British precedents in the good neighbour schemes promoted by many forces over the years[8] and in otherwise isolated force initiatives, such as the Cardiff building site reward scheme described in Appendix A. The idea is that groups of neighbours band together to act as their own and each other's 'eyes and ears'. They take note of anything suspicious and pass it on to the local police[9] and they keep an eye on one another's houses or other property. Neighbourhood watch schemes provide a convenient and economical way for police to disseminate crime prevention propaganda and to reach groups of people who ought on the face of it to be highly motivated to act on it. They encourage people to take a greater interest in physical prevention. Thus crime prevention surveys and property-marking form a major part of many schemes. Neighbourhood watch is therefore a good way of increasing the market for the standard products of physical crime prevention.

The idea behind neighbourhood watch is to heighten people's awareness of the possibility of crime occurring and to improve the scope for reducing crime by removing opportunities and increasing surveillance. Neighbourhood watch is therefore designed to appeal strongly to people's self interest. It has also been widely promoted on the grounds that it will help improve police-public relations and the quality of community life. The Metropolitan Police order which accompanied the launch of neighbourhood watch in London states that schemes can 'provide a structure to promote . . . campaigns to improve the quality of neighbourhood life'. A report on the scheme in Northumbria states: 'Neighbourhood watch is the creation or recreation of a community atmosphere' (Police Staff College, 1984, para. 2.7). A Home Office document prepared to help police officers establish and run schemes speaks of neighbourhood watch 'drawing the community together, making it more aware of its mutual dependency and responsibility' (Smith, 1984, para. 2).

The first neighbourhood watch scheme was established in Mollington, Cheshire in 1982 (see Cheshire Constabulary, undated and *Police Review*, 13 May 1983). Since then, the number of schemes has grown rapidly. By September 1984, schemes were in operation in 22 forces and there were plans to introduce them in a further eleven (Turner, 1984, Appendix B). In the Metropolitan Police, where neighbourhood watch was launched in September 1983, its growth can only be described as extraordinary. In March 1985, the Metropolitan Police gave a figure of nearly 1300 schemes in the London area, a rate of growth of three or four new schemes for every working day.

Organisation and activities of neighbourhood watch

Neighbourhood watch schemes have developed both from initiatives by local communities and by the police. The usual procedure is for a meeting to be organised following leafletting and canvassing and, in some cases, a police-initiated survey of all local residents. Local coordinators or contact persons are then selected or elected. The role of the coordinator varies according to the organisation and activities of the scheme but he or she will probably help administer the scheme, recruit new members, act as point of first contact for the police and relay information about suspicious activity to the police.

Neighbourhood watch schemes are generally seen as being most appropriate and potentially most useful in areas where there is a high incidence of the type of crime most likely to be prevented and deterred by watch activities. A high incidence of domestic burglary is usually taken as a good indicator of the need for neighbourhood watch although vandalism, theft of cars and of bicycles and street robberies have all been seen as susceptible to being deterred by neighbourhood action. Schemes are also considered to be useful where fear of crime is high, irrespective of the incidence of crime. Residents' willingness to participate is crucial: the Home Office recommends that at least 60 per cent of households in any given area need to participate if the scheme is to work well

(Smith, 1984, para. 10).

The way that schemes are organised varies considerably. Some have a formal committee structure and constitutional mechanisms for electing officers both to the committee and as coordinators. Some are built on to existing organisations such as residents' associations, an arrangement recommended by the Home Office as helping to sustain participants' interest. Others are so loosely organised that their structure is difficult to discern. The lack of an organisational blueprint has certainly allowed a degree of experimentation with different models from which it should be possible to draw some useful lessons; but it has also provoked accusations that the police are less interested in the substance than in the appearance of activity and that the foundations of many schemes have been inadequately planned and thought out (Clifton, 1984; Hibberd, 1984).

The activities of watch schemes vary too. Some require little more than that residents place stickers in their windows advertising their membership of a scheme. Others are more ambitious and include public meetings; regular newsletters; property marking; the provision of escort services, for example for those out alone after dark; liaison with victims' support schemes; bush telegraph systems for warning neighbours of suspicious activity; collective security initiatives; and lobbying for environmental improvements.

Neighbourhood watch is still in its infancy and there exists relatively little information on the various ways in which schemes have been implemented. Nor have the characteristics that make for successful schemes been identified. However the report by Avon and Somerset Constabulary on a pilot project in Kingsdown, an area of Bristol, is an excellent exposition of what is involved in neighbourhood watch from a police point of view and it also provides some information on effectiveness (Veater, 1984). A similar though less thorough evaluation of a pilot scheme in Northumbria (Millfield in Sunderland) has been prepared by students at the Police Staff College (Police Staff College, 1984). More general discussions of the philosophical and practical issues surrounding the introduction of neighbourhood watch in London are to be found in Turner (1984) and Hibberd (1984) and in the various papers prepared by the Libertarian Research and Education Trust (1984a-d). The Home Office has prepared recommendations as to best practice (Smith, 1984) and is funding a detailed evaluation of selected schemes in London.

The main claims that have been made for neighbourhood watch relate to its effects on crime. It has been widely publicised as leading to substantial reductions in residential burglary and/or crime more generally

Reductions of between 20 per cent and 50 per cent have been claimed in parts of London, in Northumbria, Sussex and Cheshire. In Kingsdown, recorded domestic burglary, theft of and from vehicles and of bicycles fell by 28 per cent during the first year of neighbourhood watch. A public survey found a drop in actual, as opposed to police-recorded victimisation of a similar magnitude (24 per cent).

It is too early to say whether these early claims will be confirmed by the findings of careful evaluative research. The figures that have been produced to date are based on recorded crime and are derived in most areas from very small numbers, so they certainly cannot be regarded as conclusive. All that can be said with any confidence is that such *prima facie* evidence as there is on the effects of neighbourhood watch on crime merits further exploration. It can by no means be assumed, however, that the infant, however vigorous it appears at present, will grow into a strong and effective adult. Neighbourhood watch, like other crime prevention measures that have initially seemed to promise much, is vulnerable to the kinds of theoretical and practical difficulties I have mentioned. It also has a few of its own. The possible displacement effects of schemes, for example, have scarcely been discussed still less systematically explored; and serious thought has yet to be given to means of keeping up the enthusiasm and morale of local participants. Nor is the philosophical basis of neighbourhood watch without its critics. For example, some have voiced the suspicion that neighbourhood watch is not so much a worthy attempt to encourage community self help as a thinly disguised drive by the police to recruit informers. Others, noting that schemes have been a good deal easier to establish in middle class, relatively low crime areas, where it is argued they are less needed, fear that neighbourhood watch will prove to be socially divisive.

The history of crime prevention teaches us that it is common for those who wish to market new initiatives to claim for them an unprecedented degree of success. Future evaluations may well show that neighbourhood watch is successful — in some circumstances if not in others. For the moment, such a conclusion is exaggerated and premature. It is also worth remembering that, so often in the past, crime prevention measures have proved stronger on promise than on performance.

Notes

1. Some other initiatives are outlined in Appendix A, but less full information is available on them than on those described in this chapter.

2. With the exception of the Home Office demonstration project, each of the projects described in this chapter was set up and run by the police. The 1984 Home Office circular on crime prevention envisages local government making more of the running in devising crime prevention strategies and initiatives (see especially paras. 15 and 16), a process which might be expected to gain momentum if preventing crime indeed becomes 'a task for the whole community'. The Home Office Crime Prevention Unit is keeping track of these initiatives. Many local authorities spend money on upgrading the physical security of estates (installing entry-phones, better lighting and so on), often as part of more general environmental improvement schemes on hard-to-let estates. (See, for example, Greater London Council, 1983b.) These schemes have as one of their aims the reduction of crime, particularly vandalism, the dropping and dumping of litter, and burglary. However, crime prevention is often only one aspect of a much broader strategy to get tenants involved in the management of their own estate and to improve amenities. Police involvement is secondary and limited to providing crime statistics and responding to tenants' requests for patrol presence. Examples of such initiatives are to be found in the various publications prepared by the Department of the Enviroment in connection with its Priority Estates Project and listed in Department of the Environment, 1982. The National Association for the Care and Resettlement of Offenders (NACRO) helps to run many similar initiatives. See NACRO, 1984; Bright and Petterson 1984; and Hedges, Blaber and Mostyn, 1980.

3. For example, the Home Office states 'concentrated efforts by the police, local schools and other community services, together with tenants . . . have much reduced the previous levels of crime on the estate'.

4. They were: the divisional chief superintendent; two juvenile liaison officers and the area constable; the head teachers of four local schools; the local vicar; the director of housing; the director of social services; and the assistant chief probation officer.

5. Very little of the crime prevention work carried out by beat officers has been documented: the various methods of collecting and disseminating information on policing initiatives described in Appendix B have overlooked this kind of work. In view of the recommendations of the working party on probationer training (Home Office, 1983b) that greater emphasis should be put on crime prevention in the training of probationary constables, there seems to be scope for maintaining some sort of national index on beat crime prevention initiatives.

6. For example, the Home Office publication, *Crime prevention: a coordinated approach* (Home Office, 1983d) and the joint circular on crime prevention (Home Office, 1984a), not only treat coordination as unproblematic, they also make claims for its success. Thus the former states: 'research has clearly shown the value of a coordinated . . . approach to crime prevention' (p. 4). The circular states: 'crime prevention schemes are more successful where the police and local agencies work together in a coordinated way' (para. 3). As I shall show, the evidence is a good deal more equivocal than these statements allow.

7. For example, the group was consulted by the city planning officer for its views on a proposed housing development. The group lacked the skills to formulate, or to convey, any clear or coherent recommendations to the city council.

8. A Home Office circular on crime prevention panels, issued in 1971, describes such schemes as 'widespread'. 'Basically they advise people what to do and what not to do when going on holiday and provide the householder with the means of getting his neighbour to keep an eye on his house and of notifying the police in his absence.' (Home Office, 1971). The main difference between such schemes and neighbourhood watch seems to be that the latter tend to be more formally constituted and organised and require more time and effort to be put into them by the police.

9. A checklist of what might count as suspicious incidents is to be found in the Home Office document, *Neighbourhood watch. A note on implementation* (Smith, 1984). It

includes: strangers walking around a residential area for a prolonged period and for no apparent purpose; persons on foot carrying valuable property; strangers engaging young children in conversation; and vehicles moving slowly and aimlessly.

6 A CAUTIONARY TALE: THE CASE OF UNIT BEAT POLICING

In his book, *Hooligan. A history of respectable fears*, Geoffrey Pearson (1983) describes how much of what modern commentators perceive as new in the patterns and potential threat of modern crime finds identical echoes in the preoccupations of whatever age we care to cast back to. Pearson is talking about modern worries over rising crime and lawlessness, but his analysis could equally well apply to the tendency to hark back to a golden age of police-public relations, often epitomised by the image of the village bobby, all-knowing, all-wise, and perfectly in tune with the temper of his local community. So far, much of this book has been about how similar images and their modern bureaucratic equivalents have been used to sustain and justify new departures in policing. The figure behind the image, however, remains an elusive one and attempts to define him, give him substance and status and see what kinds of effects he has on the behaviour and feelings of the people around him have proved to be fraught with difficulties. In this chapter, I describe how one such attempt to recreate an image and practice of policing in the late 1960s and to try to measure its effects came unstuck. The episode provides an object lesson in some of the pitfalls that can lie in wait for research on new policing initiatives. There are many lessons in it for those who are apt to find answers to policing problems in the new initiatives described in this book, and, in particular, lessons for those who look to research to provide justifications for what they would like the police to do.

In August 1967, the Home Office issued a circular aimed at encouraging forces to adopt a new system of policing, later described by Her Majesty's Chief Inspector of Constabulary in his report for that year as 'the biggest change in fundamental operational police methods since 1829' (Home Office, 1968b, p. 75). This policing system, known as unit beat policing (and described in more detail below) involved forces in additional expenditure on cars and personal radios. The purpose of the circular was to tell forces that not only was the Home Office willing to underwrite the costs of acquiring this equipment in the normal way, it was also prepared to take the unusual step of, in effect, lending police authorities the money with which to buy the necessary cars.[1] Besides offering additional grants, the circular claimed a number of other

88

seductive-sounding advantages for the new method: unit beat policing, it said, provided a rapid response to calls for police help; promoted good relations with the public; and enabled information about crime and criminals to be collated systematically and retrieved swiftly. It improved police morale and it saved on manpower.

Current wisdom has it that putting officers into cars under unit beat policing has done grave damage to the traditional relationship of trust and confidence between police and the public. (This and other disillusionments with unit beat policing are discussed below.) It has conveniently been forgotten that unit beat policing was marketed on the claim that it provided answers to precisely those ills to which it is now presumed to have given rise: inappropriate use of resources; the low status of beat officers; low police visibility; poor detection rates; poor police-public relations; and lack of public cooperation. Yet unit beat policing appeared, on the face of it, to be well researched and the claims made for it were said to have been made on the basis of such research. Indeed, unit beat policing was presented as being in large part a creation of research. With hindsight, the claims made for it may seem thin or oversold, yet at the time they proved an essential part of the official mythology of unit beat policing. So it is instructive to look at how that mythology was created, the kinds of information that were brought to bear on it and where that information came from.

The forerunner of unit beat policing was a policing scheme in Kirkby, a Liverpool overspill town which the Lancashire Constabulary found difficult to police. Kirkby had high crime and juvenile delinquency rates and although accommodation had been set aside for them when the town was built, few police officers wanted to live and work there. The result was that an area seen as posing a serious policing problem was under-policed.

This deficiency was tackled by amalgamating Kirkby's eleven existing foot beats to form five mobile beats, each patrolled 24 hours a day by a panda car. Patrol officers were issued with personal radios which enabled them to be in touch with each other and with their local station. The town centre continued to be patrolled on foot but otherwise Kirkby was policed entirely by motorised patrols.

There is no published research on the success of the Kirkby scheme though it seems to have been one. The Lancashire Constabulary extended it to two other divisions in the force, and it was variously claimed that the scheme reduced crime and increased detections, improved police morale and won accolades from the public. In a *Times* article about the scheme, the then chief constable, Eric St Johnston wrote,

In the last eight months of 1965, compared with a similar period in 1964, there was a decrease of 31 per cent in the number of crimes reported to the police, whilst the detection rate rose from 29 per cent to 37 per cent. Cases of damage fell by 53 per cent with a detection rise from 9 per cent to 21 per cent. The number of street accidents was reduced by 16 per cent. (Quoted in St Johnston, 1978, p. 169.)

The chief constable attributed these improvements directly to the introduction of motorised policing.

The Home Office Police Research and Planning Branch monitored the progress of the scheme at intervals during 1965 and 1966. Unpublished Home Office memoranda record senior officers at Kirkby as reporting 'more general awareness of police activity and a general awareness by the public that the police are doing something tangible to protect them'. It was 'noticeable that the public are more ready to pass urgent information to the police knowing that they will see a police car arrive within a very short time of their call'. There was 'no doubt that the morale of the general public had been enhanced by the emergence of much police activity'. Everyone was reported to be pleased, particularly the police, who had discovered a new sense of 'verve and eagerness' in their work. Motorised patrolling had resulted in 'several arrests' which could only be attributed to additional mobility and speedy response. Recorded crime also fell and the scheme was reported to have had a particularly marked effect on the incidence of vandalism: during the first twelve months of the scheme, the number of cases of malicious damage fell by 73 per cent, of wilful damage by 34 per cent and there was a 62 per cent decrease in the cost of damage to property.

The Kirkby scheme was followed about a year later by a modified version of it in Accrington. The brainchild of the Home Office Police Research and Planning Branch, the Accrington scheme became the model for unit beat policing, which seems to have emerged largely intact, in both conception and design, from this first experiment. The scheme aimed to combine the best of two policing worlds: the traditional idea of the country policeman (now to be imported into urban areas) plus the increased mobility and communication provided by the cars and radios used in the Kirkby scheme. Twelve foot beats became four motorised beats, patrolled around the clock. Superimposed on each car beat were two area constables, each with geographic responsibility for his own area within the beat. A detective constable was also assigned to each car beat; and an additional detective constable acted as a collator, collecting and sifting information passed to him by the beat constables and keeping them informed of anything useful discovered by their colleagues. This arrangement was to enable them all to spend as much time as possible working the beat. The essence of it was that policing an area was expected to become a team effort: 'apprehensions and other good police work are considered as the work of the team and not of the individual' (Home Office, 1967b, p. 140).

The Accrington scheme, and those that followed it, had five main aims. These were: to increase police efficiency; to improve police-public relations by providing closer contact with men on the beat and swifter response to calls for assistance; to increase and improve information flow; to overcome a shortage of police officers; and to create a new challenge in the method of beat working. According to the *Report of the working party on operational efficiency and management*[2] the scheme was devised as a response to a number of problems. Police officers were in short supply and it was difficult to find enough to patrol all the existing beats. On 1 January 1966, actual male establishments fell short of authorised strength by 7,846, or 11 per cent, and in the same year one in six forces were 20 per cent or more under strength.[3] In addition, traditional methods of foot patrol were beginning to fall into disfavour. Many patrol officers were unconvinced by the traditional deterrent rationale for foot patrol. They found themselves with little to do and had become bored and frustrated by patrol duties. They wanted higher status and felt that beat duties were regarded as inferior to work in specialist departments. The working party considered that the aimlessness and lack of incident resulting from the way patrol was organised, together with other unattractive conditions of service such as night work, contributed to premature wastage amongst constables and discouraged intelligent people from applying to join the force.[4] Therefore, some way was needed to make patrol work more interesting, to

> elevate the status of the beat constable in a way that would bring out the best qualities of a policeman — self-discipline, personal initiative and discretion — and challenge his intelligence, as well as his maturity and common sense, from the outset (Home Office, 1967b, para. 15).

As well as its effect on constables, traditional patrol was seen as having a further drawback — a less-than-positive effect on police-public relations. A training film issued to police forces and paving the way for the general introduction of unit beat policing, commented as follows on the traditional source of authority of the British policeman and its demise under the then system of foot patrol:

The fine reputation of the British policeman has always stemmed from his being the trusted guardian of law and order. Essentially, this trust has depended on the community feeling that a particular constable belongs to them. Living amongst them for a long period, they know him personally and willingly cooperate with him in his work. Knowing him as their constable, they confide in him and provide him with the information he needs to anticipate and prevent crime.

In the centre of modern towns and cities, this cooperation between public and police has been lost to a considerable degree. In contrast to the village policeman, the town centre policeman finds little opportunity to get to know members of the public. The majority of his time is entirely non-productive in terms of crime detection and of virtually no value in terms of crime prevention. His role is mainly a passive one and what action he does take is too often far removed from the prime concern of the police — the war against crime. This lack of the right communication between public and police leads inevitably to a sense of frustration in both, the former because crime incidence continues to increase and the latter because they cannot obtain sufficient cooperation to take effective action.

The case was therefore clear. The lack of appeal of the existing beat system to patrol officers, the inefficient use of manpower it involved and the inadequate service it offered to the public, constituted what the working party called a 'formidable indictment' of the existing system. What was needed now was a way of dealing with these problems, and by great good fortune unit beat policing was about to prove itself more than adequate to the challenge.

The research

. . . we stress that any experiments in so fundamental a matter as the system of policing must be evaluated by research (Home Office, 1967b, para. 23).

An important feature of unit beat policing was that, initially at least, it was to be an *experimental* system, initiated by the Home Office and evaluated by its Police Research and Planning Branch. Yet despite this, no formal evaluation was published of the Accrington scheme, nor of any of the 30 or so similar experiments which were under way by the time the Home Office issued its August 1967 circular. In the years 1965 to 1967, when the groundwork was being laid for the changes involved in introducing unit beat policing, the Police Research and Planning Branch issued only one report and two three-page articles on it. The report (Gregory, 1967) is not a research document but more of an operational *aide memoire*, providing helpful hints for forces thinking about implementing unit beat policing.[5] It contains no hard data on the effects of the new schemes, nor does either of the two articles published in the *Police Research Bulletin* (Gregory and Turner, 1967; Williamson, 1967).

This lack of publicly available data makes it difficult to assess the claims that were made for unit beat policing. These were considerable. 'Without exception', claimed the working party, 'these experiments have so far shown marked improvements in the ability of the police both to prevent and detect crime' (para. 13). Unit beat policing had been 'received with great enthusiasm by the public . . . wherever it has been tried'.[6] It had 'undoubtedly brought about a marked improvement in the image of the police' (Williamson, 1967). 'Above all' opined a senior official speaking in the Home Office training film, 'the men themselves like the new scheme. It has improved their enthusiasm and improved their morale.' Hardly surprising, since there was, according to the working party 'no doubt . . . that unit beat policing offers a more attractive, interesting and worthwhile job than the old-fashioned system of regular patrolling; it is a job that calls for qualities at least as high as those demanded by the so-called specialist branches of the service' (para. 22). And finally, there were the 'substantial economies' (ibid.) in manpower yielded by unit beat policing, variously calculated at 5 per cent, at least 10 per cent, 12 per cent, 33 per cent and 40 per cent.[7]

How all these claimed effects were achieved is not clear. The most straightforward is the claim to use available manpower more efficiently: clearly cars allow fewer officers to patrol larger areas and to visit more places more often. The falling crime and improved detection rates seem to have been attributable to two factors. First, it was claimed that cars made police more visible and hence more likely to deter potential wrong-doers: 'if . . . one conspicuous car patrols the street, it has the equivalent preventive effect of at least five uniformed men on foot'.[8] Second, the availability of an area beat officer meant that the public could pass more information to him, and the establishment of team working and particularly the post of collator, meant that this information could be used more effectively. It is less clear why the public should have been so enthusiastic about unit beat policing. Perhaps they wanted to see more police officers around and panda cars succeeded in giving this impression. Perhaps the area constables, whose job it was to follow up complaints from the public and generally show the flag, were able to provide an appropriately ubiquitous impression of helpfulness and presence. We are not told. One can also only speculate on the possible reasons for improved police morale. Cars obviously keep the cold out and the rain off; and personal radios were said to promote the feeling of being closer to help and advice (Turner, 1966). But no information seems to have been collected on how individual officers spent their time, the kinds of tasks they undertook, what they felt about those tasks, and whether unit beat policing changed any of that.[9]

Speculating about the ways in which the supposed effects of unit beat policing were achieved begs the questions of what was measured in the first place and how it was measured. Published information suggests that the measures were limited. The working party report, in a section called 'measurement of the scheme', mentions only two: recorded indictable and other 'preventable' crimes plus what looks to be an operational aid rather than an evaluative tool — a system of weighting information so as to make possible the anticipation of crime and other incidents (Home Office, 1967b, Appendix 2, paras. 10 and 11). Gregory and Turner's (1967) article adds detections; the contribution of the new intelligence system to detections; traffic offences; manpower; and the suitability of vehicles. Set against the aims of the scheme (see page 91 above) these measures hardly seem adequate. The emphasis is almost entirely on recorded crime figures, presumably because these were most readily to hand. No direct measures of public attitudes, police-public contact, police morale, police response times or police visibility appear to have been contemplated even though all these things had been presented as crucial features of the new schemes. Nor is there much information on Police Research and Planning Branch files to substantiate the claims made for unit beat policing. For example, there is nothing from which to judge public reaction to the new schemes other than occasional second-hand reports of senior officers who were invited to give their views on what the public felt about the schemes. Apart from retrospectively collected crime statistics, there are also no pre-experiment data on crucial features of deployment and operational procedures. Whatever might have happened after unit beat policing, it is difficult to assess what was going on before it and, therefore, to assess the kinds of changes which might have resulted from it. It is not possible to tell, for example, how frequently areas were patrolled, and how visible those patrols were to the public, or how action taken or information obtained by patrol officers contributed to detection before unit beat policing was implemented.

In short, available material, both published and unpublished, gives few grounds for believing that this 'biggest change in fundamental operational policing methods since 1829' was ever properly evaluated by research. Despite public statements to the contrary and the use of apparently research-based information to support the introduction of unit beat policing, it seems that virtually no research worthy of the name was carried out on it. Instead, research seems to have been relegated to a back seat under pressure to implement unit beat policing countrywide in the shortest possible time. By the time the Home Office had finalised the financial arrangements set out in its August 1967 circular and designed to encourage all forces to adopt unit beat policing, the Accrington scheme had been running for only a year. Further experiments in other forces had been in place for even less time than that. In none of these cases would it have been possible to carry out the kind of research that was needed to test the effectiveness of unit beat policing. And even if this had been possible, it is highly unlikely that unit beat policing would have emerged as the unqualified success which it was made to seem.

Research on unit beat policing then, far from being designed to test policy assumptions and to provide information to inform policy, was instead largely a fiction which was used to dress a policy necessity in the clothes of virtue. The necessity was a manpower shortage and an obviously appealing technical solution to it. The virtues were as old as policing itself: the need to restate and reaffirm the basis of consensus, the need to demonstrate determination and effectiveness in the war against crime, and the desire to instil pride in the job. These virtues are usually to be found waiting in the wings wherever policing change is in the air, and in the case of unit beat policing, the language of research was duly employed to summon them centre-stage.

Disillusionment sets in

One result of this state of affairs has been that as political winds have changed, the apparent promise of unit beat policing has not been sustained. In 1975, the Police Research Services Unit at the Home Office produced a report which looked at how areas in nine forces were being policed under unit beat policing in 1972 and 1973 (Comrie and Kings, 1975). The report identified a number of deficiencies in the way that unit beat policing had been implemented and concluded that 'the idea of the unit has not had the real operational trial it deserves' (para. 143). The authors found, for example, that in one area, unit beat policing had been implemented without any area constables having been appointed.

In no area had the idea of team work basic to unit beat policing really taken off and, in particular, CID officers and area constables had not been integrated into the teams. Panda cars were being used primarily for responding to incidents at the expense of undertaking preventive patrol and officers were failing to get out of their cars to patrol on foot. This last finding led Comrie and Kings to reaffirm the value of general foot patrol and to recommend that greater emphasis should be given to it. 'The main argument against car patrol is one of effectiveness . . . a police officer on foot is more effective a deterrent than an officer in a car' (paras. 33 and 34).

That such a finding represented a complete volte-face from the official wisdom of only a few years before goes unremarked in Comrie and Kings' report. For the low esteem in which central elements of unit beat policing are currently held stands in ironic contrast to what was initially so unequivocally claimed for it. Panda policing is now upbraided for doing precisely the opposite of what it once apparently so successfully managed to achieve. No longer is it claimed that it increases police-public contact, improves police visibility, cuts crime and raises the standing of police in the eyes of the public. On the contrary, according to most modern commentators, unit beat policing has resulted in a 'depersonalised and insensitive' system of policing (Baldwin and Kinsey, 1982, p. 97), which is 'unconstrained by local sanctions' (Kettle and Hodges, 1982, p. 67). Manwaring-White (1983) sums up a view that enjoys wide currency, both within the police service and outside it.

> The pandas were, it is widely agreed, a disaster. They distanced the police from the public and, it has been suggested, encouraged policemen to see themselves in uncomplicated terms as knights-errant in the war against crime rather than as members of the community fully bound up in all aspects of its life and so lessening the likelihood of crime occurring in the first place (p. 23).

It is not difficult to see in these kinds of pronouncements indications of precisely that attitude to evidence which characterised the introduction of unit beat policing. General claims are made about public expectations, public satisfaction and operational policing practice without these assumptions being subjected to empirical scrutiny. There is also of course much here that closely parallels the expectations which attach to many of the more recent innovations discussed so far in this book. In many of them, as with unit beat policing, a past, a present and a desired future state of affairs are constructed on claims which owe more to a political mood than to the careful collection and analysis of evidence. In this sense, the implementation of unit beat policing is much more than a historical curiosity. It is a very clear lesson on the power of a timely idea to determine how and where evidence is sought, and even to substitute for it altogether; that is, on the limitations, even irrelevance, of research-based planning in the service of policy.

Notes

1. The circular stated: 'exceptionally, where local financial resources are lacking or inadequate, the Secretary of State will himself be prepared to place contracts for the purchase of additional cars this year for delivery direct to forces against repayment by the authority as early as possible in the next financial year' (Home Office, 1967a, para. 3).

2. This and two sister working parties on manpower and on equipment were appointed by the Police Advisory Board in January 1966. The working party on operational efficiency and management had as its terms of reference:

> to review the operational organisation of the police, any non-negotiable conditions of service of police officers, and related questions of management, which bear on the efficiency and well-being of the police service of England and Wales.

Save where indicated to the contrary, all subsequent descriptions of the Accrington scheme are taken from the report of this working party. The reports of all three working parties were published together in January 1967 (Home Office, 1967b).

3. *Report of Her Majesty's Chief Inspector of Constabulary for the year 1966*, Ch. 2 (Home Office, 1967c). The figures are for England and Wales, excluding the Metropolitan Police District. Figures for women officers, who made up less than 4 per cent of force strengths, are given separately in the Report.

4. In fact, as a contemporaneous working party on manpower discovered, wastage amongst constables was no higher, or was lower, than that in other occupations for which it had information. Moreover, the working party attributed that wastage not to the boredom of patrol duty but to poor pay, unpredictable hours and to rigid and authoritarian management. *Report of the working party on manpower*, Part II, in Home Office, 1967b.

5. For example, the report talks about whether area constables should live on their beats, how long they should serve in any one area, the virtues of local versus centralised control rooms, whether patrol cars should be single or double crewed, the extent to which CID organisation might hamper cooperative team-work and so on.

6. Lord Stonham, then Minister of State at the Home Office, speaking in a House of Lords debate on crime and the community on 29 November 1967 (*Parliamentary Debates, Lords* vol. 287).

7. The working party calculated a 12 per cent saving in the manpower required to work the traditional beat system in those (unspecified) urban areas where unit beat policing had been tried. This translated into a figure of 5 per cent over the country as a whole (para. 23). Gregory's report puts the average saving at 'at least 10 per cent' of the officers currently used for beat coverage. The Home Office training film claimed that unit beat policing offered a 40 per cent saving, though the actual numbers quoted in the film translate into a saving of only 33 per cent.

8. This statement is made in the Home Office training film. Its provenance is puzzling. In 1965, the Police Research and Planning Branch undertook a series of experiments in four forces in order to test the relationship between levels of foot patrol and crime and

arrest rates. The findings are reported in *The beat patrol experiment* by J.A. Bright, which was published by the Police Research and Planning Branch in 1969. Bright's findings are not straightforward, nor is his presentation of them. He concludes, for example that 'the thesis that increasing levels of foot patrols will reduce crime is rebutted by the results of this experiment'. This conclusion is not altogether supported by Bright's findings which were that while some experimental variations in the level of foot patrol (e.g. from one to two officers per beat) failed to reduce crime, other changes (e.g. increasing the number of patrolling officers from one to three) did so. These unexamined discrepancies make it particularly difficult to assess Bright's claim that his study provides 'evidence in support of the introduction of unit beat policing'. He states that:

> In finding that increases in manpower on foot patrol to four men per standard beat did not significantly alter the crime situation, the requirement was that an even higher level of 'apparent' men per beat should be achieved. The mobile component of unit beat policing in promoting a high level of activity was to meet this requirement.

It is this statement which seems to form the basis of the claim made in the training film that one patrolling car prevents as much crime as do five officers patrolling on foot. The statement is based on two assumptions. First, that more than four officers per beat would produce a deterrent effect which the experimental increments in manning levels had not always managed to achieve; and second, that the effect of a motorised patrol was to increase perceived police visibility by at least a factor of five. Neither assumption is supported by any evidence.

9. In subsequent studies (undertaken outside the Home Office) it has been argued that patrolling in cars increases officers' opportunities to do exciting and interesting police work. (See, for example, Holdaway, 1984, Ch. 10 and Smith and Gray, 1983, Ch. III.) But such considerations do not appear to have affected those responsible for implementing unit beat policing.

7 CENTRAL INTERESTS AND CENTRAL INFLUENCES

As the previous chapter illustrates clearly, innovations and change do not just happen. They take place within a political and economic climate in which particular changes come to be seen as more or less inevitable or desirable and others as unnecessary or impracticable. Central government plays a crucial role in determining this climate and hence the direction and pace of change, and it also acts more directly in helping to market specific innovations. In this chapter I look at the formal machinery that is available to central government for influencing change and how it has been used in relation to some of the innovations described in this book. I also outline recent developments in how government has chosen to operate that machinery with a view to creating an environment which is receptive to change, and to a lesser but none the less important extent, to influencing operational priorities. Here I shall be particularly concerned with the role of Her Majesty's Inspectors of Constabulary as arbiters of what is to count as efficient policing, as expert professional advisers and as ambassadors for government policies. With some exceptions, most of the influences that central government can apply and chooses to use are indirect ones: the collation and coordination of relevant information (including research); the promulgation and dissemination of best practice; and the issuing of (sometimes strongly worded) formal advice. In relation to the kinds of policing innovations discussed in this book, carrots have tended to be more important than sticks in the process of creating change. Hence this account reflects the perceived virtues of persuasion and consensus in achieving desired results.

The statutory framework

The statutory framework which defines the constitutional relationship of central government to local constabularies is laid down in the Police Act 1964. The concept of efficiency lies at the heart of this relationship. Section 4 of the Act[1] places a duty on individual police authorities to 'secure the maintenance of an adequate and efficient force for the area'. But as provider of one-half of the costs of the police[2] the Secretary of State also has a direct interest in the nature and quality of local policing.

99

This interest is defined by section 28 of the Act, which requires that he 'exercise his powers . . . in such manner and to such an extent as appears to him to be best calculated to promote the efficiency of the police'. To this end, other sections of the Act provide him with a number of permissive and regulatory powers: to require the amalgamation of forces; to force the retirement of a chief constable 'in the interests of efficiency'; to ratify senior appointments; to make regulations on the administration and conditions of service in forces; to call for reports from a chief constable on any matter to do with policing in his area; to provide certain common services such as training; and to undertake 'research into matters affecting the efficiency of the police'. The Secretary of State also has the power to apply financial sanctions by withholding grant aid to any police authority where he is not satisfied that the police area is efficiently policed or the police service efficiently and properly maintained, equipped and administered.[3] In determining such matters he is advised by Her Majesty's Inspectors of Constabulary (HMIs), who have a duty under section 38 of the Police Act to inspect and report to him on the efficiency of forces. It is on the basis of these reports that, in practice, individual police authorities qualify for receipt of specific grant. In addition to their inspectorial functions, HMIs must also 'carry out such other duties for the purpose of furthering police efficiency as the Secretary of State may from time to time direct'. In practice this means interpreting and commenting on the local scene for central government and acting as ambassadors for government policies.

Although the Police Act signals very strongly central government interest in policing and provides the Secretary of State with a number of direct and indirect ways in which he can affect it, the relationship of the Home Office to the police service is an ambiguous one whose content and meaning has changed in response to political and economic circumstance. This ambiguity is an inevitable consequence of the failure of the Act to define certain key terms and relationships. Thus although the relationship of the Secretary of State to local constabularies is defined in terms of the former's duty to promote police efficiency, the Act nowhere defines what efficiency is nor does it give any indication as to how its meaning and content might be derived. The Act is similarly vague on the nature of the distinction between the responsibilities of the three parties to it and on the rights and duties of each. Under section 5, the chief constable is made responsible for the 'direction and control' of his force. The Act does not define these terms but historically the chief constable has been seen as being solely responsible for decisions to enforce the law in particular cases with neither the police authority nor the Secretary of State having any locus in this matter.[4] The extent of a chief constable's operational autonomy in other matters (for example, his general policies on law enforcement, his policing priorities and decisions about how to allocate and deploy resources) is, however, much less clear. The 1962 Royal Commission on the Police clearly envisaged that a police authority's relationship to its chief constable on questions of operational policing ought to differ from its relationship in respect of law enforcement in particular cases. The Commission's view was that a chief constable ought not only to be 'exposed to advice and guidance' from his police authority, he ought also normally to be expected to follow it.[5] The Police Act, however, fails to say where police authorities stand on this. It does not preclude them from offering advice, but it fails to make specific provision for it. Nor does it place any obligation on a chief constable to follow his police authority's advice and it gives police authorities no powers to make their advice stick. In practice, therefore, the extent to which advice is offered and is seen to have legitimacy and authority depends very largely on the particular working relationship between an individual chief constable and his police authority.

Whatever a police authority's locus in matters of operational policy and priorities, the Act gives them clearly defined provisioning duties. The authority is responsible, subject to the approval of the Secretary of State, for setting force establishments; with the consent of the Secretary of State, for providing buildings; and for providing equipment. By implication, therefore, an adequate and efficient force is, at the very least, one that is properly equipped and staffed. The difficulty here is that definitions of adequacy and efficiency presuppose some notion of what it is the police are there to do and some standards by which these tasks can be judged to have been done. It is therefore difficult to see how any hard and fast distinctions can be maintained between *what* is spent on policing (for which police authorities are clearly responsible) and *how* it is spent — an operational issue where a police authority's responsibilities are, in other respects, much less clear. The idea (discussed below) that police forces ought to give 'value for money' must erode this apparent distinction even further through its attempt to inform policy by making explicit the links between resources which can be costed (inputs) and what, in operational terms, is achieved for that expenditure (outputs).

The locus of responsibility for determining operational priorities is further complicated by the Secretary of State's duty to promote police efficiency. Whilst this duty clearly overlaps with that of police authorities to maintain an efficient force, the Secretary of State's responsibility to satisfy himself that police authorities are complying with their statutory duty as a condition of payment of exchequer grant means that in practice his definition of what constitutes efficiency is likely to be an overriding one. How the Secretary of State chooses to define efficiency is therefore crucial. The Police Act of course offers no guidance, so that what constitutes efficient policing is, in effect, left entirely to the Secretary of State to determine. He may define it as narrowly or as broadly as he wishes and in relation to whatever criteria he chooses. It is clear that the definition of efficiency can be drawn in such a way as to give the Secretary of State considerable scope for affecting operational policies and operational deployment: the development of unit beat policing is one such example. Equally, the Secretary of State may define efficiency so vaguely and so loosely as to give him very little purchase on operational priorities. As with matters of expenditure, it is a mistake to regard issues of efficiency as purely technical or administrative ones. Instead, efficiency is potentially a highly political construct whose meaning and components change over time and which will be defined more or less explicitly in accordance with the influence which the Secretary of State wishes to exert on policing policy. Changes in the definition of efficiency therefore provide an important barometer of central government interest in operational policing.

Although the Secretary of State has an unfettered discretion to determine what should count as operational efficiency, the nature of his powers means that he is not often in a position to enforce his views directly. Both the grant sanction and the power to require the resignation of a chief constable in the interests of efficiency are drastic penalties which are unlikely to be seen as appropriate save in extreme circumstances and to remedy gross defects. Moreover, such punitive sanctions are ill-suited to the more general development of policing policy and good practice and to the encouragement of innovation. This is more likely to thrive in an atmosphere of support and encouragement than under conditions of threat. The creation of such an atmosphere, and of conditions in which his views and advice will be seen as influential — even authoritative — ought therefore to be an important concern of any Secretary of State wishing to affect the nature and direction of policing policy. His permissive powers — for example, to offer advice, fund research and provide training — provide him with considerable resources for doing this, should he choose to use them.

Home Office circulars

One important resource available to the Secretary of State is the circular. These provide a formal and symbolically effective means of communicating to forces central government views and information it wishes them to take note of. The Home Office issues between 100 and 200 such circulars each year. Most of them are no more than descriptions of new legislation, administrative regulations and their effects. However, circulars are on occasion also used to communicate the state of Home Office thinking on certain policy issues and to encourage forces to follow Home Office advice. Circulars are therefore one means of stimulating innovation in forces.

Circulars can help to stimulate innovation in a number of ways. They may simply disseminate information on Home Office policy or on what other forces are doing in the hope that it will be taken note of and motivate action. More positively, circulars may endorse what is thought to be good practice and exhort forces to adopt it. In both cases it is important, if they are to have desired effects, that circulars should be seen by their recipients as having something worthwhile to say. An important aspect of this lies in the extent to which circulars help to articulate and formulate a policy consensus. Most advisory circulars therefore are not issued until those at whom they are aimed (for example, the Association of Chief Police Officers) have been consulted about their contents.

The fact that such consultations take place must make it more difficult for individual chief constables to hold out against Home Office advice. In addition, although circulars are in theory 'advisory' and the penalties (if any) for not complying with them often left vague, their heavily didactic tone is frequently indistinguishable from an instruction to conform to what they recommend. In particular, circulars employ a range of devices designed to maximise the probability of their being complied with. These range from financial incentives, as in the circular with which the Home Office induced forces to implement unit beat policing, to implied financial penalties, as in circular 114/1983 (see below), which threatens to refuse force requests for manpower if they fail to pursue and demonstrate best use of existing resources. More subtly, forces may be asked to respond to the advice contained in a circular by specifying what they intend to do about it; and this response may later be followed up with a further circular asking them to state how far their intentions have been realised. Some crime prevention circulars have employed this device: for example, the circulars aimed at encouraging the growth of crime prevention panels and the Ditchley circular (see Chapter 4).

Many of the innovations described in this book can be linked to Home Office circulars. This does not mean that by themselves circulars can create innovation and change where this would otherwise be unwelcome or unlikely. They are, however, important in articulating ideas which have already begun to gain currency and thus in giving both a sense of direction and a boost to change. Like definitions of efficiency, the number and content of advisory circulars provide an important barometer of the extent to which central government feels compelled and able to take a hand in influencing operational priorities.

The willingness of the Home Office to use circulars and other resources to try and affect policing policy changed a great deal during the period over which this review was prepared. The Home Office has raised its public profile on policing: it has taken a greater interest in what goes on in forces and has put more effort into trying to affect it. Two factors have contributed to the development of this more interventionist stance. The first was the riots in 1981, which marked a turning point in the Home Office's relationship with forces. Many forces looked to the Home Office to provide help and guidance in dealing not only with the immediate political consequences of the riots, but also with their longer term effects. The dominant ethos within the department — that operational priorities were largely a matter for chief constables to determine without reference to the centre — changed markedly as the Home Office took advantage of a more receptive local climate to extend its influence over a wider operational territory. The proper definition of and limits to a chief officer's operational independence have, as a result, become more narrowly drawn; and there is also a greater acceptance by forces of the inevitability of such a change, though not necessarily its desirability.

The second development affecting the relationship of the Home Office to forces is the squeeze on public expenditure and, in particular, articulation of the idea that the police service must give 'value for money'. This has raised a set of questions which, although not new in themselves, have become much more explicitly and consciously formulated. The need to raise these questions has heightened Home Office awareness of how limited is its knowledge of what goes on in forces, and in particular of where policing expenditure goes and what are the returns on it. In seeking this information and in taking a direct interest in what the products of policing are, the Home Office has been drawn into a new set of relationships with forces and has signalled very clearly its interest in what forces do and how well they do it: in other words with operational priorities.

Both the riots and the squeeze on public expenditure have direct consequences for the kinds of innovations described in this book. Following the riots, there has been renewed emphasis on re-establishing and
revitalising old consensual traditions and embodying them in new institutional forms. Expenditure restrictions have introduced a new language
of management accounting into discussions of policing policies and policing priorities. In the remainder of this chapter I describe how this
language is affecting definitions of efficiency and of what constitutes 'best
practice' in policing; and how ideas about what counts as best practice
are formulated and disseminated through the work of Her Majesty's Inspectors.

Adequacy and efficiency: defining terms and operationalising them

Although they have an important place in the way in which the accountability of the police is formally secured, the terms adequacy and efficiency have never been precisely formulated or defined. Instead they
have functioned as convenient (and elastic) terms whose meanings have
changed as policy preoccupations have changed. The introduction of a
language of management accounting into policing means that definitions
and measures can no longer be fudged, as has tended to be the case in
the past. Thus an adequate force is one which performs the tasks it is
supposed to perform and an efficient force performs them at least cost.
Measures of adequacy and efficiency imply some definitions of what it
is the police are expected to do and some standards by which those tasks
can be judged to have been done. In theory then, determining efficiency
ought to be a deliberate analytical exercise.

In the early 1970s there was an ill-fated attempt to come to grips with
these issues by devising and applying a system of output budgeting to
policing, but this seems to have left little trace on current practice. Apart
from that attempt, it is only recently that much thought has been given
to trying to systematise and make explicit the basis of judgements about
adequacy and efficiency.

Efficiency and the role of HMIs

The Police Act designates Her Majesty's Inspectors of Constabulary as
the main arbiters of efficient policing. Inspectors' main statutory duty
is to inspect and report on the efficiency of forces. This is done annually.

There are currently five HMIs,[6] based regionally, each of them responsible for inspecting between six and ten forces.

The format and content of inspections have never been statutorily defined nor administratively regulated but have evolved out of custom and practice. The annual inspection process begins with a series of information-gathering activities and culminates in a formal, set-piece visit by HMI. Inspectors go armed on these visits with a considerable amount of statistical and other information (submitted to them each year by forces) on operational strengths and deployments, recruitment and promotion; and a pre-inspection report, prepared by a staff officer in the inspectorate, commenting on developments since the last inspection and laying out particular issues which ought to be pursued and policies which need to be reviewed. During the inspection visit, which lasts for three to six days and is therefore of necessity somewhat ritualistic,[7] the inspector will meet senior officers of the force to discuss aspects of policy and he will usually see members of the police authority who may also accompany him on his visit. He will visit different parts of the force, and will make spot checks of relevant files and paperwork.

Inspectors submit two reports, neither of which is published. A short preliminary report provides a general assessment of the organisation, management and morale of the force. The main inspection report draws together information on manpower, administration, equipment, crime and operational policing and ends with the inspector's judgement on whether or not the force is efficient. (He invariably finds that it is.) Before 1983, when their format changed, inspection reports were almost entirely descriptive. In their flavour, tone and content they were not unlike the annual reports of chief constables and those of Her Majesty's Chief Inspector. The descriptive material they contained was presented largely free of an analytical context and without inferences being drawn from it. Because they were so short on analysis, it is difficult to tell from the reports alone what it is about force organisation and performance that leads inspectors to their judgements about efficiency. Inspectors themselves find it hard to articulate the basis of their judgements. Perhaps this is because these judgements are not made *de novo* each year but in relation to a history of past judgements, which would be difficult to gainsay. If a force was judged to be efficient last time round and nothing too dramatic has gone wrong in the meantime, then it is difficult to see how an inspector can avoid finding it efficient this time round. Thus judgements about efficiency are effectively negative ones, to do with the absence of anything untoward, rather than positive ones about how force administration, or procedures, or particular operations measure up to specified criteria. Given the low priority that has been given to thinking about policing performance and how this might be assessed, it is difficult to see how this situation could have been otherwise.

The financial management initiative

Since 1983 the format and content of inspection reports have changed and inspectors have begun to work to more explicit guidelines in determining what should count as efficiency and in probing force performance. The background to this development is the government's financial management initiative. This requires government departments to have

a clear view of their objectives and means to assess and, wherever possible, measure outputs or performance in relation to those objectives;
well-defined responsibility for making the best use of their resources; including a critical scrutiny of output and value for money;
and the information (particularly about costs), the training and the access to expert advice that they need to exercise their responsibilities effectively.

In addition:

where practicable, performance indicators and output measures will be developed which can be used to assess success in achievement of objectives . . . The question departments will address is 'where is the money going *and* what are we getting for it?' (HMSO, 1982, paras. 13 and 15. See also HMSO, 1983 and 1984.)

Because the police service accounts for over two-thirds of the 80 per cent of Home Office expenditure which is incurred by local authorities, and because expenditure on the police has risen considerably in real terms, the Home Office has chosen to concentrate on the police service as part of its contribution to the financial management initiative.

The initiative has several strands. It includes an attempt to devise performance measures for police, a financial information system for HMIs, and new-look inspections. Behind all of these is an attempt to get individual forces to retune their thinking in line with an atmosphere of resource constraint rather than one of hoped-for expansion and to encourage forces to engage in critical self-evaluation.

Thinking about performance and grappling with outputs

The idea that police performance not only ought but also can be assessed and measured more adequately than has been done in the past underlies my discussion of virtually all the force initiatives described in this book. The search should be for measures which are relevant to readily definable objectives and which will remove some of the ambiguity and wishful thinking that characterises the presentation of much what passes for policing innovation. It is therefore impossible to talk about measures of police performance (or the related concepts of output, effectiveness and efficiency) in the abstract. What are deemed to be appropriate measures will depend on who is devising them and for what purposes, and on the extent and ease with which different sorts of information about performance can be made part of systems of incentive or control. Central government will have an idea of measures of performance different from an individual constable thinking about how best to work a beat, or from a crime prevention officer wanting to know whether a property-marking scheme is worth the effort. And a government aiming to control levels of expenditure may want different measures from one trying to determine 'ideal' levels of provision or standards of service. Although the financial management initiative has implications for the ways information is collected and analysed at all levels of a force, it is primarily concerned with providing information to government. Government is concerned mainly with expenditure decisions (that is, the question 'where is the money going?') and the financial management initiative also requires it to ask 'what are we getting for this money?' Government is also concerned to advance particular policies. It therefore needs information which will help it to think about expenditure in functional terms, as well as information to help it judge how certain policy goals have been achieved. In doing both of these things the Home Office has chosen to continue to rely heavily on the professional judgements of HMIs but to provide them with new sorts of information to help them apply that judgement.

Financial information

Police budgets are drawn up under heads which bear little relationship to the main kinds of activities the police perform. They break down broadly into: employment costs (which constitute upwards of 80 per cent of the total); day-to-day running costs; revenue contributions to capital; and debt charges. These broad classifications are then further sub-divided: for example, running expenses into premises, transport, supplies and services and so on. For anyone wanting answers to the question 'where is the money going?' in terms of what it is the police actually do, the budget is clearly an unsatisfactory starting point. It is even more so in relation to the question 'what are we getting for what we spend?'

Under the financial management initiative the Home Office has set out to classify and allocate police expenditure according to functional categories rather than traditional administrative ones. The categories, which are then further sub-divided, are: patrol, public order, crime, community relations, traffic and other operational activities; and training, management and other non-operational activities. By requiring expenditure to be classified in this way, both HMIs, and through them, the Home Office, hope to be able to assess whether resources are being allocated 'in line with national and local priorities' (HMSO, 1984, p. 70) and to make comparisons between different force expenditures and thus encourage accounting for any apparent inconsistencies.

The financial information system has a precedent in a 'planning, programming, budgeting system' (PPBS) introduced experimentally by the Home Office in the early 1970s into twelve forces. The rationale and purpose of PPBS provide some uncanny parallels to the financial management initiative.[8] The then Home Secretary described his interest

in encouraging the development of a management information system for the police . . . to try to relate the cost and performance sides of the management problem in a systematic and orderly way; [and] to provide those in the public services who are responsible for the employment of large shares of our scarce national resources with a precise and relevant store of information for their job of management and planning . . . [A] management information system . . . can provide the managers of our public services with more and better information and a sounder framework for making these judgements. It produces a budget in which all expenditure is organised in functional blocks according to the activities and objectives of the service concerned. (The Rt Hon James Callaghan, speaking in November 1969, quoted in Christian, 1982, p. 6.)

Under the PPBS experiment, the following functional categories were devised: ground cover (which included patrol); crime investigation and control; traffic control; additional services; management; overhead programmes; training; and support services. (See Wasserman, 1970, who also describes further breakdowns in each category.) Yet despite the fact that the PPBS experiment ran for five years, little progress was made in creating its other main plank and its central rationale: output measures which related to the broad functional categories into which policing expenditure had been divided. The experiment folded in 1974 when the Home Office no longer required forces to submit to it financial information classified by policing function.[9] The participating forces could have continued with the scheme had they wished to do so but none of them felt that the benefits of the new costing system were such as to encourage them to persevere with it in the absence of central government interest. Their disappointment seems to have derived mainly from the failure of central government to make much headway in specifying detailed policing objectives (as opposed to functional categories of expenditure) and in devising measures of policing performance which could indicate whether or not those objectives were being achieved.

The Home Office intends that the financial information system currently being devised for HMIs will eventually be linked to some measures of police performance. It remains to be seen whether this can be done. It is no accident that the PPBS experiment foundered on this particular rock. Since then, a decade of policing research has served only to demonstrate how tenuous is the relationship between resource levels and even relatively straightforward and measurable policing objectives such as the reduction of crime. A report on effectiveness and efficiency measures, commissioned by the Home Office as part of its response to the financial management initiative, reaches much the same conclusion in finding few, if any, global statistical measures which can be used as unambiguous measures of police performance (Sinclair and Miller, 1984). Scepticism about the possibilities of devising overall performance measures is also apparent in the Home Office's expressed intention to continue to rely on the professional judgements of HMIs in reaching conclusions about the efficiency of police forces. Financial information will simply alter the context in which these judgements are formed.

On this view, the application of financial information is unlikely to become a way of establishing what is the 'best' or most effective use of police resources. It is instead a way of presenting existing information in new forms such that a different, more analytical and more empirically based set of questions can be addressed to it. It helps to provide a method of questioning, a structure within which questions can be asked and a vocabulary of accounting, all of which to tend to stress the importance of demonstrable achievements over conventional assertions. As such, it forms part of a larger package designed to encourage better management of resources through a greater commitment to empirical methods. New-look inspections and a Home Office circular, *Manpower, effectiveness and efficiency in the police service*, issued in 1983, form the other main elements of this package.

Home Office circular 114/1983

Circular 114/1983 heralds a 'new outlook' on resource management (Collins, 1985, p. 75) and thus on the way policing priorities are set and are to be judged. To begin with, the circular gives formal notice (in appropriately circumspect language[10]) of the government's intention to cut back on recent rates of growth in police expenditure; and it lays down a framework within which forces wanting to apply for increases in establishments will be expected to advance their claims, and a series of criteria to guide them. Equally importantly, it introduces a highly specific language of rational management into the process of determining policy priorities. The circular emphasises the need for forces to set 'objectives and priorities' and defines what they ought to take into account in doing so. It seeks to promote a more questioning style of management within forces and stresses the importance of regular internal review. And it encourages forces to formulate 'good practice' based on careful assessment of their own initiatives. In addition, the circular gives some substance to what constitutes efficiency. Instead of being the absence of anything untoward, efficiency is expected to be determined by reference to certain informational criteria which are themselves based on a clearly articulated idea of what the force is trying to achieve. Thus resources should be allocated 'in a way that will most effectively and efficiently secure [force] objectives and priorities' (para. 5); while 'the effective and efficient use of resources . . . depends crucially on knowledge of where and when they are most likely to be needed and what results they will have . . . [R]esources should be applied on the basis of what they are likely to achieve' (para. 10).

All this of course presupposes a considerable capacity within forces for collecting and analysing relevant information in testing for effectiveness and efficiency. The circular sets out to encourage such an approach both by stating and restating the need for it and by suggesting how it might be developed. Forces are therefore urged to research their own initiatives, to disseminate the lessons they learn from this, and to undertake major reviews of their policies. The circular draws attention to the availability of help from HMIs and to outside research assistance, and to the importance of describing and evaluating force practice in such a way that others can learn from it.

New-look inspections

The circular gives HMIs a key role in helping to achieve the aims set out in it. In particular, the requirement to account in the language of objectives and of demonstrable achievements has been made an explicit part of the inspection process. Inspections have become more analytical and probing and the inspector's role has become not only a much more overtly proactive one but also much more closely and explicitly linked to the policy concerns of the Home Office. Inspections are now conducted within a framework of more explicit guidance which specifies what the Home Office wants to know about what forces are doing. Since 1984, forces have been required to submit more detailed, systematic and purposefully organised information to HMIs before the latter make their formal inspections. The information required for 1985 covers 23 separate areas of Home Office interest, grouped under three main heads: activities (essentially operational matters), management and manpower.[11] In essence, four different sorts of information are required from forces: written descriptions of what is happening; supporting descriptive statistics; information on the sorts of self-monitoring and assessment systems that a force has; and information about the effectiveness of various activities. Under crime prevention, for example, forces are asked to give details of new initiatives, including those undertaken in conjunction with other specified agencies; the extent to which patrol officers and not just crime prevention officers are involved in giving crime prevention advice; and how and whether new initiatives and patterns of crime in the force are monitored and with what results. In relation to deployment of manpower, forces are asked amongst other things to specify how changes in deployment have helped to meet force objectives; and how and whether patrol officers are directed as to how they should spend their time and with what results.

These new-look inspections have some important implications. Most significantly, they require forces to think about their activities and to produce evidence for their effectiveness in ways which, on much of the evidence of this book, may cause them considerable difficulties. Many of the questions which the Home Office is now posing through the inspectorate presuppose a capacity to take stock which, in practice, is built into relatively few policing activities and operations; and they create a demand for analysis which forces are not particularly well-equipped to respond to. More explicitly focused inspections also give the Home Office access to more, and more detailed, information about what is going on in forces and hence a more adequate basis than has perhaps existed hitherto for determining (and thus helping to disseminate) what constitutes best practice.

HMIs' advisory role and the dissemination of best practice

HMIs are not only responsible for reporting on force efficiency. Over the years they have also taken on increasingly important advisory functions such that formal inspecting no longer constitutes the major proportion of their work. The 1962 Royal Commission on the Police took note of what it called the constructive functions of inspectors: 'the encouragement of initiative in individual forces and the sharing of new ideas or practices between one force and another, [and] more particularly the responsibility for forward thinking about the demands of executive policing over wider areas than those of individual forces' (para. 245). The Commission recommended that this function be developed further. HMIs were to become responsible for advising on arrangements for promoting collaboration between forces, for ensuring that the results of government research were made available to the police and that new knowledge and up-to-date techniques were being applied. The intention was that, by acting as purveyors of information to forces and identifying successful local initiatives and spreading the word about them, inspectors would come to act as catalysts to innovation. HMIs were referred to rather charmingly in this context in a subsequent parliamentary debate as acting 'just like bees fertilising flowers'.[12] In circular 114/83, the importance of this aspect of HMIs' work is restated. They are expected to be key figures in the business of identifying and disseminating good policing practice.

The idea that good policing practice can be identified and forces encouraged to adopt it raises questions about the role and status of HMIs and their relationship to the Home Office and the police service. HMIs need a foot in each of two camps: that of central government and that of operational policing. Their status as civil servants means that they are bound to act as ambassadors for government policies. Equally, as professional advisers to government, they can expect to be able to exert influence on those policies. Inspectors' influence with the police service is obviously affected by the administrative sanctions they can set in train if forces fall far short of minimum efficiency. But the limitations of those sanctions in respect of large areas of policing policy and practice mean that inspectors have little more to fall back on than their professional status and standing and the fact that they are accepted as having something worthwhile to say. The framework of assumptions within which they operate is therefore crucial. If they are to be persuasive, inspectors cannot afford to be too far out of line with police service thinking. The prestige of the inspectorate and the personal qualities of the inspector are important too. Inspectors are appointed from the ranks of chief constables. (The appointment is regarded as promotion.) They are therefore fairly closely tied, by virtue of their direct and recent experience of it to the world of operational policing — experience which is bound to help them in establishing credibility and authority with forces.

The other side of this coin is the limitations that inspectors' experience places on their capacity to exercise a truly independent judgement. This is not just a matter of their professional history. In trying to reach conclusions about what constitutes good practice, inspectors are very dependent on information presented to them by forces and, as I have shown, this information is often partial or inadequate. The inspectorate seems to have set little store on developing an analytical capacity of its own and in common with many of their operational colleagues, HMIs appear indifferent to the messages of a lot of policing research.[13] The avowed intention to use inspectors as one of the main means for identifying and disseminating good practice has not been backed with adequate resources. It is ironic that as inspectors' advisory role has expanded, the annual reports of the chief inspector show that the number of inspectors and assistant inspectors with functional responsibilities has declined. The publication of the report of the Royal Commission on the Police in 1962 led to an expansion of the inspectorate and by 1964 there were eight regional inspectors plus an assistant inspector responsible for women police.[14] By 1982, the number of regional HMIs had declined to half its 1964 level, despite a 50 per cent increase in force establishments over the same period,[15] and there were two assistant inspectors with functional responsibilities (respectively for computers, communications, management and information systems and research and training; and crime, traffic and community relations). In 1983, an additional regional post was created.

Because of its small size, the inspectorate has been unable to develop the kind of public profile which distinguishes, for example, the work of Her Majesty's Inspectors for education. In disseminating good practice, inspectors of constabulary work almost entirely behind the scenes.

They have directly contributed very little to public debate. The inspector's public face is largely limited to the annual publication of the report of its chief inspector, who tends to avoid distillations of collegiate wisdom in favour of reporting a considerable volume of descriptive statistics and more general exhortatory pronouncements related to government policy. The report for 1983, for instance, endorses the sentiments of circular 114/1983, contributes to the rehabilitation of crime prevention and commends neighbourhood watch, civilian-staffed administration units and schools liaison programmes as methods of advancing police effectiveness. It also continues the tradition of previous years of selectively reviewing (without critical comment) preventive policing projects.

It is not easy to tell from this kind of information how inspectors feel able to recognise good practice when they see it, how they persuade forces of the virtues of experimenting with and adopting new ideas and how actively they are, or feel they should be, involved in the processes of initiating, facilitating and managing change. An annual report is not necessarily the best place in which to consider such matters in detail; the difficulty is that the inspectorate publishes little else. It appears instead to favour the professional grapevine both as a way of identifying good practice and as a means of disseminating it. Here again, comparison with inspectors of education is instructive. The latter, like inspectors of constabulary, have become increasingly involved in central government policy-making. Unlike inspectors of constabulary however, inspectors of education have regularly published state-of-the-art reviews, surveys of exisiting practice and accounts of the kinds of practice they would wish to encourage,[16] thereby helping to stimulate debate and discussion within the profession and outside it. Possible subjects for such treatment in relation to policing might include the place of women in policing, ethnic minority recruitment, or even, to follow the example set by the education inspectorate in its publication *Ten good schools, Ten good crime prevention departments.*

There is, of course, no shortage of issues in policing that would merit systematic study and comparison by critically inclined professionals. If the idea is to be taken seriously that HMIs should be in the forefront of determining good practice on the basis of good information, and of encouraging forces to develop such practice themselves, changes will need to be made both to the assumptions within which the inspectorate operates and the resources which are put at its disposal.

Notes

1. These statutory provisions do not apply in the Metropolitan Police District, where the Home Secretary acts as police authority. His statutory relationship to that force is governed by the various Metropolitan Police Acts.

2. Unlike most other local government services, the police service is funded directly by central government. Half the cost of the police is found by local government and half by central government.

3. These and other conditions which have to be met before a police authority qualifies for exchequer grant are listed in article 2, Police (Grant) Order 1966.

4. The Police Act 1964 does not refer specifically to law enforcement (nor does it use the term operational autonomy). However the 1962 *Final report* of the Royal Commission on the Police, from whose recommendations the Police Act grew, was clear that in relation to law enforcement in particular cases, chief constables' discretion should be unfettered (paras. 86–7). For a description of how this position has evolved, see Jefferson and Grimshaw, 1984, especially Ch. 2.

5. Para. 93. Moreover, a chief constable who 'persistently disregarded and flouted such advice' would bring his fitness for office into question.

6. This figure excludes the Commandant of the Police Staff College (whose post is ranked as HMI), the Chief Inspector and two assistant inspectors with functional as opposed to geographical responsibilities. The size and composition of the Inspectorate is described in more detail on page 114.

7. There is an instructive contrast here with the length of visits undertaken by Her Majesty's Inspectors for education in inspecting schools. A team of HMIs may spend up to several weeks in each school. It is of course much easier — and makes rather more practical sense — to observe the work of teachers in classrooms than officers on patrol, or wherever. The education inspectorate is also much larger than the inspectorate of constabulary. There are about 460 inspectors in the former, a ratio of one inspector to approximately 1200 teachers (Department of Education and Science, 1982, Table 7.2). The ratio of inspectors of constabulary to provincial police officers is one to 20,000.

8. This account of PPBS is taken from Christian, 1982.

9. The reasons for the Home Office withdrawing from the scheme are described in Christian, ibid., 136ff and 200ff.

10. The circular speaks of the desirability of a 'period of consolidation' following the rapid growth in police expenditure of the previous decade or so.

11. The full list is as follows:

Activities
Crime prevention; relations with the community; operations against crime; Police and Criminal Evidence Act; treatment of victims; prosecutions; public order; traffic; warning and monitoring system.
Management
Organisation and structure; information systems; technical services; training; personnel management and career development; complaints and discipline; relations with staff associations; relations with police authorities; buildings.
Manpower
Deployment of police manpower; manpower planning; recruitment; civilian staff; special constabulary.

12. Lord Brook of Cumnor, speaking in a House of Lords debate on crime and the community, November 1967 (*Parliamentary Debates, Lords*, vol. 287, col. 115).

13. The annual reports of the Chief Inspector contain a chapter on scientific and technical research and services within the Home Office. The policing research by the Home Office

Research and Planning Unit rarely rates a mention.

14. Until the Sex Discrimination Act 1975, women police officers formed a separate branch of the service and were also inspected separately. The post of inspector for women police was abolished in 1979 when its incumbent retired.

15. HMIs had, however, fewer forces to inspect in 1980. In 1964 there were approximately three times the number of forces in England and Wales than there are now. Against this, the ratio of regional inspectors to provincial police officers changed from 1:8,000 in 1964 to 1:23,000 in 1980.

16. See Department of Education and Science, 1982, Appendix C, which lists 39 publications in the eight years from 1973.

8 POLICING BY OBJECTIVES OR BY SUBJECTIVES?

In this chapter I shall try to bring together the evidence and trends I have reviewed so far in order to discuss the place of 'planning' in policing and the extent to which the rational collection and assessment of evidence can stand as a model for assessing what the police do and how well they do it. From the schemes and changes I have reviewed so far I shall try to identify some of the incentives and disincentives to making greater rationality a major component of police thinking and of police management styles. Finally I shall look at some of the obstacles to introducing rational planning and by implication a whole variety of innovations and changes into policing. Such a discussion has to be both general and speculative. One of the notable features of most of the available documentation of policing initiatives is how little it has to say about change as a process, with all its attendant irritations, compromises and backtracking; about how change is managed and about how and why it can fail. As a result, very little is known about the conditions which favour successful innovation and those which hinder it. This is an argument for more careful monitoring not just of the outcomes of new initiatives but also of the processes of implementing them.

A number of explicitly rational and information-based models of analysis and decision-making have been described so far. In Chapter 4 I described situational analysis as a method of tackling crime prevention problems and evaluating the results of crime prevention initiatives. In Chapter 7 I looked at the interests of central government in encouraging the more rational management of policing resources and how it has tried to tighten up old forms of internal and external accounting and devise some new ones. Immediately below I describe two further models of rational management: policing by objectives (pbo) and the problem solving approach to policing.

Policing by objectives

Pbo is a thorough-going attempt to apply a rational/empirical approach to any, or all aspects of a force's activity. It is an American import and has been adopted wholesale as an approach to thinking about and

118

organising policing activity in two forces: the Metropolitan Police and Northamptonshire.[2] Although pbo has been implemented on the initiative of the chief officers of those forces, it has parallels in central government ideas about what constitutes 'best practice' in policing, particularly in its emphasis on performance measurement and on a consultative philosophy of management.

The importance of pbo lies in its mechanics and in its supporting philosophy. Stated simply, the mechanics are based on the notion of a planning cycle which has four different stages. The cycle begins with the preparation of a 'mission statement' (or force policy statement) — some general guidelines about what the force intends to do. Next comes a 'goal statement', a rather more refined statement of mission, and this is followed up by the specification of various objectives, derived from the goals and forming 'the heart of the PBO planning process' (Lubans and Edgar, 1979, p. 87). Finally come the action plans — specifications of what needs to be done. In 1983, the Metropolitan Police Commissioner specified six goals for the force to pursue that year.[3] Under the first of these goals (to do with crime prevention) were listed 18 objectives including increasing patrol, directing foot patrols, upgrading the status of beat constables and coordinating a multi-agency approach to prevention. The action plan for the last of these objectives reads as follows: 'to identify those other agencies . . . who could assist the police in the prevention and reduction of crime' and 'to prepare and circulate directions . . . to harness the efforts of those agencies . . . to designing out crime; situational prevention; crime specific problem solving; victim support and the promotion of positive values and standards'. As can be seen, each successive stage in the planning cycle involves greater specificity of purpose. It also involves progressively lower levels of the police hierarchy in defining and deciding what is to be done. Thus while the chief officer and, in the United States, his political masters, define the mission at the most general level, deciding what work will be done on the ground (that is, formulating the action plans) is left to the working groups who will be implementing those plans. The pbo cycle culminates in an 'impact assessment' (or empirical evaluation) of the action plans. In relation to the action plan described above, the proposed evaluation includes assessment of the cost of liaison and coordination, and changes in the number of agencies cooperating with the police. In the light of such assessments, the force objectives, goals and mission statement are subsequently reassessed and revised. The planning cycle can thus begin again.

An important feature of pbo is its dynamism. The pbo philosophy assumes that the pursuit of greater policing effectiveness is a realistic and desirable goal. Under pbo, change — or at the very least, the prospect of it — becomes an organisational way of life. Although it is not necessary (nor is it often possible) to subject all organisational activities to the scrutiny of the pbo planning cycle, in those parts of the organisation which are involved, no-one can escape from its logic. This is because pbo is more than a set of tools for analysing the purpose, nature and results of policing activity. It is also based on a management philosophy and style which emphasises the decentralisation and democratisation of decision-making. Under pbo, those who will do the work are not only to be consulted about what should be done, they become active participants in formulating it. The justification for this is that when people have been involved in planning change which affects them, they are more likely to be committed to carrying it through. By this means, pbo seeks to overcome what is often considered to be the main obstacle to implementing changes in policing: resistance from below.

Another important feature of pbo is its uncompromising emphasis on the importance of results. 'The PBO philosophy is that police activities are only as good as the results they produce, and *have no value in themselves*' (Lubans and Edgar, p. 17, emphasis added). With pbo, nothing is sacred; the unthinkable can be thought. All value judgements are suspended until activities have proved their empirical worth. Pbo abhors fudging and uncertainty. Officers in forces operating pbo have to know (or at least be able to say) exactly where they want to go, why they want to go there, how they are going to get there and when they have arrived. In essence this means setting precise and measurable objectives on the best possible knowledge of what the problems are. It is an argument for good research as a precondition of good policing.

Problem-oriented policing

Like policing by objectives, the problem-oriented approach to policing has been more extensively developed and used in the United States than in Britain (see Goldstein, 1979; Goldstein and Susmilch, 1981a for the theory and Goldstein and Susmilch, 1981b, 1982a, b for the practice).[4] It stems from the view that the police have been more interested in how they do things than in what those things achieve; in other words, that they have concentrated on questions of organisational efficiency at the expense of those of organisational effectiveness. The approach sets out to return to the purposes of policing as a starting point for discussion about what the police ought to be doing, by addressing those problems we ask, or expect, them to deal with. Like situational crime prevention, problem-oriented policing emphasises the importance of specificity in defining problems and the role of research in doing so. It is analytical and methodical. It requires:

> identifying . . . problems in more precise terms, researching each problem, documenting the nature of the current police response, assessing its adequacy and the adequacy of existing authority and resources, engaging in a broad exploration of alternatives to present responses, weighing the merits of these alternatives, and choosing from among them (Goldstein, 1979, p. 236).

It is one of the main assumptions of this book that there is much to be gained and learned from analysing more carefully the purposes and effects of changes in policing methods. It is also one of my main arguments that the police (and others) have often failed to do this adequately or even at all. Thus, although many policing initiatives start from a general recognition that all is not well or that 'something needs to be done', this is rarely carried through into a thorough and detailed analysis of exactly what the problem is as a prelude to deciding what ought to be done about it. The premium put on the desirability of innovation (in, for example, some Home Office circulars) means, as a result, that new initiatives often look like solutions searching for problems.

If policing problems are often ill-formulated in the first place, so too are the proposed solutions to them. The police have often found it hard to articulate to themselves and to a wider public what the limits to police action are and so have found themselves trying to sustain an illusion of competence virtually irrespective of the results they do or can achieve. The ambitions and targets that are set for many policing schemes reveal a naïve (and increasingly insupportable) faith in the capacity of the police to improve their effectiveness with what is often a very limited range of strategies. Thus relatively small changes in policing complements, or in the mix of car and foot patrols, have been expected to improve police-public relations and increase public satisfaction with police. Reductions of crime across the board have been sought using broad brush strategies, such as more patrolling, which take little account of the disparate nature of crime, the different circumstances in which crimes occur or the capacity of the police to affect those circumstances. And assumptions have been made about the availability of 'resources within the community' without necessarily specifying what those resources are or what police actions, if any, can or should be made to elicit them. As for evaluation, the importance of setting 'precise and measurable' objectives has been apt to take second place to acts of faith. Reports of many policing initiatives sidestep or ignore crucial problems of effectiveness or fail to collect relevant evidence about it.

Policing by objectives is a conscious attempt to remedy some of the deficiencies in planning and evaluation described in this book. Whether it (or other models of rational planning) is likely to succeed depends on a number of obstacles being overcome. Some of these exist within the police service, others come from outside it.

One obstacle is the lack of analytical skills within forces and the low status that such skills often have. If this lack is to be remedied, forces will have to attract or identify the right people, train them properly, and provide them with the organisational backing they need. Even apparently simple problems can pose considerable analytical difficulties; indeed, identifying the precise nature of the problem — an essential first step — may itself be half the battle. Thereafter relevant information (which is often not readily accessible) needs to be sought out or collected; this is often difficult, tedious and time-consuming. The analysis chosen needs to be appropriate to the quality and type of information. Finally the conclusions that follow — if there are any — need presenting in an open-minded and honest way without excessive regard for whom they might offend.

Merely acquiring relevant skills and creating suitable machinery is not, however, enough. If rational analysis is to be more than a fig leaf, the police service as a whole will have to begin to understand its discipline more adequately than it seems to do already, and begin to take on its habits of thought. This is unlikely to happen readily in a culture deeply devoted to action and its rewards. Compared with analysis, action is rough and ready, stimulating and various. It requires a sense of commitment which is undermined by the sort of scepticism which is the stock-in-trade of the analyst. The latter is therefore easily seen as an unwelcome intruder into the 'real world' and his products unrecognisable to those whose day to day experience is of the immediate and particular.

While commitment can be harnessed in the service of analysis, mere faith cannot. One of the main conclusions of this review is that preconceived ideas about what needs to be done have distorted the way in which evidence of change is collected, interpreted and presented. A great deal of discussion of policing innovations has an evangelistic quality to it which makes the innovations unusually difficult to evaluate rationally. This is not difficult to explain. Policing draws its legitimacy from the sacred aspects of tradition and a great deal of the kind of policing innovation reviewed in this book can be viewed as a reworking of those aspects in new institutional forms. The value of concepts like 'prevention', 'collaborative effort', 'community' and 'public acceptability' lies precisely in their appeal to these sacred aspects: they have a powerful legitimating function. To question the appropriateness of such concepts is thus to question the legitimacy to which many innovations make appeal and so may appear fundamentally subversive of the very purpose to which they are directed. It is, therefore, hardly surprising that much of the research on policing innovation to date has failed to keep a critical distance from what it sets out to evaluate but has instead become an integral part of the process of legitimating policing activity. In other words, instead of guiding policy, research has conformed to its demands. If this explanation is correct, it does not bode well for the future of rational analysis of policing.

Models like policing by objectives, with their uncompromising emphasis on the importance of results, together with central government efforts to encourage greater performance-consciousness by the police may, ironically, exacerbate rather than put a brake on the tendency for police research to find what it is looking for. Rational analysis is a two-edged weapon. A more realistic view of what can be achieved by policing innovations may be less attractive than it seems. The police are right to ask that they should be judged accountable for the right things to the right degree, and rational analysis is, on the face of it, a powerful tool for establishing what the boundaries to the possible are. But a more realistic idea of what the police can achieve will not necessarily reduce the pressure on them to present themselves in the best possible light. The public seek reassurance and it has been an unfortunate tendency of that research which has been properly conducted to undermine the basis on which that reassurance has been given. Without greater public understanding of, and tolerance of, the limits to police effectiveness, police presentations of those limitations are likely to be seen as excuses for failure. The tendency to gloss may thus be reinforced.

Despite the developments I described in Chapter 7, there is so far little evidence that central government is prepared to make a consistent effort to increase public understanding or to follow through the logic and consequences of some of its own policies. Demands for better performance measurement sit uneasily with some of the claims being made (without supporting evidence) for the success of other policies to which the Home Office appears committed and which it is urging the police to adopt. For example, the Home Office has stated that one result of the kinds of reviews which circular 114/1983 exhorts forces to carry out is that police effectiveness has been improved (Home Office, 1984b, p. 12). It claims that crime prevention is one of the most cost effective ways of achieving greater public confidence in the criminal justice system (ibid., p. 10). There is virtually no evidence that either of these statements is true.

These kinds of statements indicate that rational analysis is viewed not so much as a method for discovering the truth as a means to an end whose efficacy has already been decided. It is as if, in encouraging the police to look more objectively at their own activity, the government has thoughtfully provided them with a description of what they should see. Once again, it is the policy which is the horse and research the cart.

The claims of research can never be more than modest. The claims of important institutions, however, may need to be something more. One of the attractions of policing by objectives (and similar models) is that it is based on the premiss that the claims of institutions need to be brought back down to earth. The extent to which the application of rational methods will be allowed to influence the direction of policing policy will be a test of the commitment of the police service and politicians to something less rhetorical and compelling than a policing ideal.

Notes

1. Advocates of pbo in this country take as their bible the book *Policing by objectives. A handbook for improving police management* by V.A. Lubans and J.M. Edgar. The description in the text of pbo is taken from this source.

Policing by objectives was published in the United States in 1979. Its principal author has visited England to advise on pbo schemes here and has also influenced the management courses taught at the Police Staff College. A recent do-it-yourself guide for British police managers (Butler, 1984) draws heavily on its philosophy and practical guidelines.

2. Other forces have adopted parts of pbo. See, for example, the Merseyside Police document, *Planned policing* (Christian, 1983).

3. These were:

i.   to reduce criminal opportunity by developing police resource management, police/community cooperation and contact improved order maintenance

ii.   to maintain and improve police capability for controlling disorder, but with a more economic use of resources

iii. to increase the detection of street robbery and burglary by reorganising and concentrating detective manpower; by coordination of other relevant manpower resources and by upgrading the status and quality of intelligence collation, targeting and surveillance

iv.   to maintain the present performance of squads centrally employed against organised and specialist crime, but with less manpower

v.   to maintain the present standard of police performance in regulating traffic and law enforcement, but with less manpower

vi.   to shape and control demand for secondary services.

Report of the Commissioner of Police of the Metropolis to the Home Secretary. Action Plans, January 1983. A condensed version of these plans appears as Appendix 31 to the *Report of the Commissioner of Police of the Metropolis for the year 1982*.

4. In his report for 1983, the Metropolitan Police Commissioner refers to four pilot studies of the problem-solving approach to crime and anti-social behaviour. The four studies, each in a different area of London, are of racial attacks, shoplifting, motor vehicle crime and prostitution.

APPENDIX A

POLICING SCHEMES

NAME OF SCHEME	FORCE	AIMS OF SCHEME	MAIN FEATURES OF SCHEME	EVALUATION MEASURES	STAFFING AND COST IMPLICATIONS
Luton Area Policing Experiment March–September 1981 (extended countywide in November 1981)	Bedfordshire Police	to provide preventive policing more in keeping with community needs, wishes and problems to reduce incidence of crime, especially vandalism, in areas with a high proportion of young people to provide a better service, thus increasing the flow of criminal intelligence. (Stonecliffe, 1983, p. 6)	Appointment of 16 area constables and 5 sergeants to cover 5 areas with a brief to attend incidents not requiring immediate response and develop close links with schools, youth clubs etc Establishment of a police surgery in each area.	Police statistics on workload and deployment Interviews with community members Interviews with police officers; observation of patrols.	Not known

Sources: Stonecliffe, M.H. (1983) *An Evaluation of the Luton Area Policing (Experiment)*, MSc Thesis, Cranfield Institute of Technology, Department of Social Policy. Chief Inspector Marlow (1982), 'Residential policing in Bedfordshire', in Males, Stephen J. (ed.), *Initiatives in police management*, Police Research Services Unit, Home Office, London.

NAME OF SCHEME	FORCE	AIMS OF SCHEME	MAIN FEATURES OF SCHEME	EVALUATION MEASURES	STAFFING AND COST IMPLICATIONS
Derby East Community Policing Experiment 1982–	Derbyshire Constabulary	to improve police effectiveness to increase public satisfaction to make officers' jobs more rewarding. (Parrish, 1983, p. 43)	Pre-existing complement of 170 sub-divisional officers reorganised into 4 area teams Reduction in number of cars Provision of a 'police surgery' in each area Officers 'devise their duties to meet the demands of the area they police' 1 week's community relations training for all participating officers.	Police statistics on recorded crime and detections, arrests, cautions, road accidents, calls for service, police vehicle mileage, complaints against police Public opinion survey Survey of attitudes of police officers.	No additional officers required Additional training amounting to 204 officer weeks 33% reduction in number of vehicles and 7% reduction in annual mileage in first year of scheme.

Sources: Parrish, A.S. (1983) 'Community policing. The Derby East Police Scheme', *Australian Federal Police Journal*, December. May, Doreen (1982) 'The Derby East policing experiment', *Police Review* 16 July. Parrish, A.S. (undated) *Derby East policing experiment. History, analysis and evaluation*, Derbyshire Constabulary.

NAME OF SCHEME	FORCE	AIMS OF SCHEME	MAIN FEATURES OF SCHEME	EVALUATION MEASURES	STAFFING AND COST IMPLICATIONS
Crime Prevention Support Unit 1976-1983	Devon and Cornwall Constabulary	to examine facts and statistics so as to identify crime problems and community problems	Crimes analysis	Interviews with police officers, agency workers and volunteers.	Not known
		to experiment with new crime prevention initiatives	Setting up of Community Policing Consultative Group, a multi-agency group with a brief to promote social crime prevention		
		to harness public support in teaching good citizenship and preventing crime.	Inter-agency placements, involving police, probation and social services		
		(Blaber, 1979, p. 10)	Provision of play schemes for young people.		

Sources: Blaber, Ann (1979) *The Exeter Community Policing Consultative Group*, NACRO. Moore, Colin (1978) *From crime statistics to social policies*, Devon and Cornwall Constabulary. Moore, Colin and Brown, John (1981) *Community versus crime*, London, Bedford Square Press.

NAME OF SCHEME	FORCE	AIMS OF SCHEME	MAIN FEATURES OF SCHEME	EVALUATION MEASURES	STAFFING AND COST IMPLICATIONS
Exeter Joint Services Youth Support Team 1979–	Devon and Cornwall Constabulary	to coordinate efforts to combat juvenile delinquency to record and analyse referrals for criminal offences and other actions to develop more effective prevention and treatment to develop community and volunteer services to support statutory services. (Morgan, 1980)	Joint working of police, probation and social services in a combined unit.	Reoffending statistics, workload statistics Interviews with team members, police officers, and magistrates.	Not known. Some Urban Aid funding.

Sources: Morgan, Brian J. (1980) *Summary of a comparative study on a new approach to combat juvenile delinquency in urban areas — case studies on Chicago, Hanover and Exeter*, Paper to UNESCO Colloquium on human rights and urban environment, Paris, 8–11 December 1980. Arnold, Jon W.D. (1983) *Exeter Joint Services Youth Support Team, Interim Report*, University of Exeter, Department of Sociology, Unpublished.

NAME OF SCHEME	FORCE	AIMS OF SCHEME	MAIN FEATURES OF SCHEME	EVALUATION MEASURES	STAFFING AND COST IMPLICATIONS
Two Parishes Project 1979–	Gloucester-shire Con-stabulary	to improve the quality of life in the area through involvement of residents in the affairs of their own community to interest official and voluntary bodies in supporting the efforts of community members to cultivate awareness on behalf of young people, that they can contribute to community wellbeing to prevent crime, especially by young people. (Butler, 1982)	Multi-agency approach involving police, probation and social services Provision of community facilities, including advice centre and youth club.	Police statistics on juvenile crime Interviews with residents Interviews with representatives of participating agencies.	Not known

Source: Butler, T. (1982) *Two Parishes Project — results and prospects. A report for the project management committee*, Gloucestershire Social Services Department.

NAME OF SCHEME	FORCE	AIMS OF SCHEME	MAIN FEATURES OF SCHEME	EVALUATION MEASURES	STAFFING AND COST IMPLICATIONS
Havant Policing Scheme 1981–	Hampshire Constabulary	to cultivate closer contacts with the community	Less vehicle patrol and more foot patrol	Police statistics on deployment and workload, and recorded crime.	Not known
		to enhance status and job satisfaction of local beat officers	Rearrangement of shifts to match manpower availability with demand for service		
		to achieve better disciplined response to public demand.	Reduction of paperwork		
		(Hampshire Constabulary, 1981)	Introduction of computerised incident logging system.		

Source: Hampshire Constabulary (1981) *The Havant policing scheme*, Winchester, Chief Constable's Office. Also reproduced in Males (1982b).

NAME OF SCHEME	FORCE	AIMS OF SCHEME	MAIN FEATURES OF SCHEME	EVALUATION MEASURES	STAFFING AND COST IMPLICATIONS
The Grange Project 1979– (selected features force-wide from 1984)	Humberside Police	to develop cooperation between the police and other services responsible for dealing with juveniles in activities which might help prevent anti-social behaviour to establish a central clearing house to collate and disseminate information to help children at risk to regard the project as a pilot scheme, with a view to implementation elsewhere in the force to monitor activities and review their effects.	Police visits to all juveniles coming to police notice Schools liaison Provision of community facilities and environmental improvements.	Police statistics on juveniles coming to notice, recorded crime and other incidents Interviews with representatives of participating agencies.	Not known – but home visit programme unable to be implemented force-wide because of manpower implications.

Table continued

NAME OF SCHEME	FORCE	AIMS OF SCHEME	MAIN FEATURES OF SCHEME	EVALUATION MEASURES	STAFFING AND COST IMPLICATIONS
The Grange Project (contd)		to consult with tenants' associations, parent/teacher associations and other organisations which might make a meaningful contribution			
		to increase juveniles' awareness of their responsibilities towards society			
		to create a better community spirit among residents			
		to reduce juveniles' anti-social behaviour			
		to reduce the number of offences committed by juveniles			
		to reduce re-offending by juveniles coming to notice for the first time.			
		(Humberside Police, undated, pp. 3–5)			

NAME OF SCHEME	FORCE	AIMS OF SCHEME	MAIN FEATURES OF SCHEME	EVALUATION MEASURES	STAFFING AND COST IMPLICATIONS
Sheppey Interagency Project 1982–	Kent Constabulary	to enhance the relationship of the police and other agencies with the local community	Schools liaison	Police statistics on number of juveniles coming to notice and juvenile crime.	Not known
		to improve liaison and understanding between local agencies and identify areas of interagency cooperation	Improved juvenile liaison		
			Provision of community facilities, particularly for juveniles.		
		to attempt to reduce local crime within the community, primarily that involving juveniles and young adults			
		to assess the need for further community resources.			
		(Kent County Constabulary, 1984, p. 441)			

Source: Kent County Constabulary (1984) *Annual Report 1983*.

NAME OF SCHEME	FORCE	AIMS OF SCHEME	MAIN FEATURES OF SCHEME	EVALUATION MEASURES	STAFFING AND COST IMPLICATIONS
Skelmersdale Coordinated Police Experiment	Lancashire Constabulary	to determine capability of uniform patrol to carry out preventive policing	Pre-existing complement of 69 officers reorganised into 4 area teams and split	Police statistics on recorded crime and detections	Initial savings of 37,000 vehicle miles per year.
1979– (extended to Blackburn in 1980)		to maintain adequate emergency response	approximately 50/50 into 'structured patrols' and shift-based response teams	Interviews with key community figures	
		to achieve flexibility in order to redeploy resources.	Emphasis on returning structured patrol officers to foot duties, with a brief to carry out preventive policing through increased community contact	Interviews with police officers; observation of structured patrols.	
		(Brown, 1981, p. 2)	Reduction of paperwork		
			Introduction of computerised incident-logging system.		

Sources: Brown, John (1981) *The Skelmersdale coordinated police experiment*, Cranfield Institute of Technology, Department of Social Policy. Laugharne, A. (1982) Skelmersdale coordinated policing experiment, in Males, 1982b. Yates, R. (1981) *An assessment of the Skelmersdale split-force coordinated policing experiment*, MSc thesis, Cranfield Institute of Technology, Department of Social Policy.

NAME OF SCHEME	FORCE	AIMS OF SCHEME	MAIN FEATURES OF SCHEME	EVALUATION MEASURES	STAFFING AND COST IMPLICATIONS
Highfields Community Policing Scheme 1976–	Leicestershire Constabulary	to enhance and improve the relationship between police and public	Increased beat patrolling by community constables.	Police statistics on recorded crime and detections; complaints against police	Not known
		to reduce tension in the area		Interviews with participating officers and their colleagues	
		to improve officers' self-image by providing greater responsibility and flexibility of action on patrol		Interviews with key community figures.	
		to reduce delinquency			
		to improve information flow between police and public			
		to improve police effectiveness.			
		(Pollard, 1979)			

Source: Pollard, B. (1979) *A study of the Leicestershire Constabulary's Highfields community policing scheme*, MSc thesis, Cranfield Institute of Technology, Department of Social Policy.

NAME OF SCHEME	FORCE	AIMS OF SCHEME	MAIN FEATURES OF SCHEME	EVALUATION MEASURES	STAFFING AND COST IMPLICATIONS
Neighbourhood Policing 1981–	Metropolitan Police (Brixton, Notting Hill, Kilburn and Hackney) Surrey Constabulary (Camberley, Addlestone and Walton)	to increase 'community helping behaviour' and stimulate community involvement in crime prevention to reduce street crime to increase public satisfaction with police to decrease public demand for response policing to decrease people's fear of crime. (Beckett and Hart, 1981 and Metropolitan Police, 1983)	Pre-existing shift-based reliefs reorganised to give them geographical responsibility Stimulation of community based and multi-agency crime prevention initiatives Introduction of participatory management at station level Rearrangement of duties to match manpower availability with demand for service.	Police statistics on recorded crime, juveniles coming to notice, racial attacks, demands for service, deployment statistics, sickness records Public surveys, including incidence of victimisation (Nott. Hill & Camb. only); survey of community leaders; analysis of press coverage Survey of police officers Patrol observation (Nott. Hill & Camb. only)	4-day training course for all participating sergeants and constables. Police implementation and evaluation team of up to 27 people.

Table continued

NAME OF SCHEME	FORCE	AIMS OF SCHEME	MAIN FEATURES OF SCHEME	EVALUATION MEASURES	STAFFING AND COST IMPLICATIONS
Neighbourhood Policing (contd)				Observation of process of implementing change in the station; observation of process of implementing neighbourhood watch.[a]	

Note: a. A large-scale evaluation is being carried out by the police themselves and the Metropolitan Police has set up a special unit to do this. The project is also being independently monitored by the Police Foundation. The list of evaluation measures does not distinguish between these two sources.

Sources: (select bibliography) Beckett, Ian and Hart, James (1981) *Management summary of neighbourhood policing*. Hart, James and Beckett, Ian (1981) *Outline of evaluation principles in neighbourhood policing*. Hart, J.M. (1982) *Neighbourhood policing. An outline description of the police station computing facilities associated with the neighbourhood policing project*. Hart, J.M. and Beckett, I. (1983) *The neighbourhood policing project. The experimental design and evaluation appraisal*. Metropolitan Police (1983) *Neighbourhood policing. Data gathering at police stations. A practical guide*. Metropolitan Police (1984) *The neighbourhood policing project. Data sources*. Metropolitan Police (1984) *Planning for a police station*. All unpublished papers, Metropolitan Police, A2(3) Branch.

NAME OF SCHEME	FORCE	AIMS OF SCHEME	MAIN FEATURES OF SCHEME	EVALUATION MEASURES	STAFFING AND COST IMPLICATIONS
Thetford Project 1983–	Norfolk Constabulary	to reduce the incidence of juvenile crime.	Situational crimes analysis Multi-agency approach to prevention; details to be decided in light of crimes analysis.	To be decided.	Not known

NAME OF SCHEME	FORCE	AIMS OF SCHEME	MAIN FEATURES OF SCHEME	EVALUATION MEASURES	STAFFING AND COST IMPLICATIONS
Felling and Scotswood Security Projects 1979/80 (Felling) 1980 (Scotswood)	Northumbria Police	to reduce incidence of burglary to reduce people's fear of crime. (Allatt, 1984a, p. 100)	Upgraded security (door and ground floor window locks) fitted to all dwellings on 2 difficult-to-let estates.	Police statistics on recorded burglary, recorded robbery and theft (Scotswood experiment only) Public survey, including incidence of victimisation, anxiety and worry about crime.	Cost (unspecified) of crime prevention surveys of 213 dwellings in Felling and about 800 in Scotswood. Security hardware costs of £10,000 (Felling) and £27,000 (Scotswood), provided by Inner City Partnership.

Sources: Northumbria Police (undated) *Prevention of fear. Part I Felling.* Northumbria Police. Allatt, Patricia (1984a) Residential security: containment and displacement of burglary, *The Howard Journal of Criminal Justice,* vol. 23, no. 2. Allatt, Patricia (1984b) Fear of crime: the effect of improved residential security on a difficult-to-let estate, *The Howard Journal of Criminal Justice,* vol. 23, no. 2.

NAME OF SCHEME	FORCE	AIMS OF SCHEME	MAIN FEATURES OF SCHEME	EVALUATION MEASURES	STAFFING AND COST IMPLICATIONS
Milton Keynes Patch Policing Experiment 1981	Thames Valley Police	to monitor incidence of crime and vandalism to enable sufficient officers to spend time in the area on foot and to make direct and sustained contact with all members of the community to give responsibility of policing to a team of officers, to the exclusion of other duties to ask public what they want from the police and how well the police functioned. (Hill, 1983)	An 8-officer team given responsibility for 24-hour policing, on foot and cycle only, and with a brief to get involved in schools and youth clubs and to get to know local residents.	Police statistics on recorded crime General public survey plus survey of key community figures Interviews with participating police officers.	Not known

Sources: Hill, T.J.W. (1983) *The Thames Valley Police Milton Keynes Division Patch Policing Experiment*, MSc thesis, Cranfield Institute of Technology, Department of Social Policy. Hall, A.S. (1981) *Strategies against vandalism*, MSc thesis, Cranfield Institute of Technology, Department of Social Policy, Appendix C.

NAME OF SCHEME	FORCE	AIMS OF SCHEME	MAIN FEATURES OF SCHEME	EVALUATION MEASURES	STAFFING AND COST IMPLICATIONS
Cardiff building site reward schemes Early 1980s	South Wales Constabulary	to reduce damage to and theft from building sites to prevent injury to trespassers to minimise delay in construction to prevent interference with plant and machinery.	Involvement of building trade, school children, teachers and residents in a 'community watch' on large construction sites Donation of £100 to each participating school by construction companies if aims achieved Opportunity to educate children in accident and crime prevention.	None known	Not known

Source: Hall, A.S. (1981) *Strategies against vandalism*, MSc thesis, Cranfield Institute of Technology, Department of Social Policy.

NAME OF SCHEME	FORCE	AIMS OF SCHEME	MAIN FEATURES OF SCHEME	EVALUATION MEASURES	STAFFING AND COST IMPLICATIONS
Property Protection Project Nov 1983–Nov 1984	South Wales Constabulary (Caerphilly)	to reduce burglary to aid identification of stolen property and increase amount returned to owners to increase police/public contact and thus improve police/public relations	Ultraviolet pens and engravers distributed free to approx 2,000 households, who then displayed window stickers advertising that their property had been marked.	Police statistics on reported burglary	Ultraviolet pens donated free by manufacturer and engraving styluses by Post Office. House-to-house visits made by special constables.

Source: Laycock, Gloria (1985) *Property Marking: a deterrent to domestic burglary?* Crime Prevention Unit Paper 3, Home Office, London.

NAME OF SCHEME	FORCE	AIMS OF SCHEME	MAIN FEATURES OF SCHEME	EVALUATION MEASURES	STAFFING AND COST IMPLICATIONS
Chelmsley Wood Policing Experiment April 1982–March 1983	West Midlands Police	to increase amount of foot patrol to release officers from response duties for structured patrol work to ensure adequate response cover to grade calls more effectively to increase flexibility of working hours and duties to make more officers responsible for a single geographical area to promote team working to enhance consultation between supervisors and their staff to reduce specialist roles to reduce paperwork. (Scientific Research and Development Branch, 1984, pp. 20–2)	Pre-existing complement of response officers and permanent beat officers reorganised into 3 structured patrols, each with geographical responsibility Evaluation undertaken with aim of providing a blueprint for evaluating all other policing schemes.	Police statistics on deployment, overtime, vehicle mileage, recorded crime, detections, road traffic accidents, process reports Public survey, including incidence of victimisation Survey of police officers' opinions and analysis of their activities.	None

Sources: Butler, A.J.P. and Tharme, Karen (1982) *Social survey — Chelmsley Wood sub-division*, West Midlands Police. Butler, A.J.P. and Tharme, Karen (1983) *Chelmsley Wood Policing Experiment*, West Midlands Police. Scientific Research and Development Branch (1984) *Report on a method for evaluating policing experiments and its application to the experiment at Chelmsley Wood, a sub-division of West Midlands Police*, London, Home Office.

NAME OF SCHEME	FORCE	AIMS OF SCHEME	MAIN FEATURES OF SCHEME	EVALUATION MEASURES	STAFFING AND COST IMPLICATIONS
Lozells Project 1980–1985	West Midlands Police	to develop links between the police and the community	Provision of funding for community initiatives, including a police-staffed youth club and a residential summer holiday camp	Police statistics on recorded crime	Approximately £250,000 provided by police (25%) and Inner City Partnership (75%) to fund community activities. Additional staffing costs unknown.
		to encourage people living in the area to participate with local agencies in solving problems within the community	A schools liaison programme.	Survey of school children, including cognitive mapping	
				Observation of and interviews with Project Steering Committee members	
		to give support to the numerous groups and agencies working within the community who strive to improve the quality of life		Interviews with community leaders	
				Social needs survey	
		through the operations of the above to reduce crime and vandalism.		Observation of and interviews with permanent beat officers.	
		(Cumberbatch *et al.,* 1982)			

Sources: Cumberbatch, Guy, Walker, Erroll and King, Gill (1982) *The Lozells community policing project,* Unpublished report to the Home Office. See also Brown, John (1982) *Policing by multi-racial consent. The Handsworth experience,* London, Bedford Square

APPENDIX B

SOURCES OF INFORMATION ON POLICING INITIATIVES

Information of the kinds of initiatives outlined in this book is also available from many other sources. These range from national data bases to short reviews of a few schemes. Below are listed alphabetically the main sources of information with some indication of their range and depth of coverage, and how to obtain them.

Annual reports of chief constables. These briefly document force projects, particularly those with a community relations slant, and usually give some indication of their perceived success. The section on research and development may also contain relevant information, particularly on efficiency initiatives. Obtainable from individual constabularies.

Annual reports of Her Majesty's Chief Inspector of Constabulary. Since the mid-1970s these have contained a short chapter on preventive policing and community relations which provides a brief description of up to a dozen initiatives with a community relations emphasis from around the country. Published by HMSO.

Cranfield Institute of Technology, Cranfield, Bedford, MK4 0AL. The Institute's Department of Social Policy offers an MSc in applied social policy. The course is aimed at practitioners and attracts several police officers each year. Their theses on policing, many of them full descriptions and evaluations of resident beat officer and other community-oriented policing schemes in students' own forces, are lodged in the Institute's library.

Crime Prevention News. A 'who's doing what' in the crime prevention world, aimed mainly at force crime prevention departments. A good source of information on local problems, small crime prevention projects and national news and campaigns. Published quarterly. Obtainable free of charge from Room 133, Home Office, Queen Anne's Gate, London SW1H 9AT.

Department of Education and Science. In 1983 the department published a survey by Her Majesty's Inspectors of Schools of police links with schools. The survey documents a number of crime prevention initiatives aimed at young people. It is called *Police liaison with the education service* and is available free of charge from Room 2/11, Department of Education and Science, Elizabeth House, York Road, London SE1 7PH.

Department of the Environment Priority Estates Project. The Project was set up in 1979 to experiment with ways of improving living conditions on difficult-to-let local authority housing estates. It includes various crime prevention initiatives. Local authorities involved in similar initiatives and Project working papers are listed in *Priority estates project 1982. Improving problem council estates: a summary of aims and progress*, obtainable free of charge from Department of the Environment, Room P2/050, 2 Marsham Street, London SW1P 3EB.

Home Office Crime Prevention Centre, Police Headquarters, Cannock Road, Stafford ST17 0QG. The Centre has recently begun to compile an index of force crime prevention schemes culled mainly from the minutes of crime prevention panels. Descriptive material is brief.

Home Office Crime Prevention Unit, 50 Queen Anne's Gate, London SW1H 9AT. The Unit is compiling (from 1984) an index of force crime prevention projects, with an emphasis on central government and local authority initiatives. The Unit is concerned to identify and disseminate best practice from a strong research base. It publishes a series of crime prevention occasional papers.

Home Office Police Research Services Unit (PRSU), Horseferry House, Dean Ryle Street, London SW1P 2AW. The Unit's Information Desk keeps a computerised index of force projects, designed for and aimed mainly at force research and planning departments. Projects are classified under the following heads: command and control; computer systems; crime; administration; operations; organisation; social sciences; equipment; miscellaneous; and traffic. Some community policing-type initiatives are included in the index but there is little specifically on crime prevention. Fairly brief information is stored on each project; enquirers are expected to follow up on particular initiatives with individual forces. A quarterly Information Desk Bulletin is circulated to forces. It is not available outside the police service. The *Police Research Bulletin*, published twice a year reports on current police applications of science and technology and occasionally contains articles of wider interest, for example, on crime prevention. *Initiatives in police management. Experimentation in the more effective use of police resources*, edited by Stephen Males, contains descriptions and evaluations (of varying emphasis and detail) of projects in 12 forces, many of them with a community policing slant. Like the *Police Research Bulletin*, it is free of charge and can be obtained from the above address. A further volume is planned.

Home Office Research and Planning Unit (HORPU) Annual Research Programme. The 1985–86 programme lists 21 projects on crime prevention and policing which are either being carried out, or funded externally by the Home Office. The programme also lists Home Office Research Studies (published by HMSO); and Research and Planning Unit Papers, which are free of charge and obtainable from HORPU, 50 Queen Anne's Gate, London SW1 9AT.

Home Office Scientific Research and Development Branch Annual Research Programme. This lists research being undertaken and funded externally by the Branch, almost all of which is concerned with police applications of science and technology. It contains a list of reports by Branch staff published over the previous year. The reports are free but, like the annual research programme, are not widely distributed outside the police service. They can be obtained from Scientific Research and Development Branch, Horseferry House, Dean Ryle Street, London SW1P 2AW.

Home Office. Crime prevention: a coordinated approach. An annex to this report lists about 20 crime prevention initiatives under the headings 'police/community crime prevention initiatives'; 'provision for juveniles'; and 'initiatives in tackling priority estates' (see also under Department of Environment). The report is free from Home Office Crime Prevention Unit (q.v.).

NACRO (National Association for the Care and Resettlement of Offenders), 169 Clapham Road, London SW9 0PU. The work of NACRO's Crime Prevention Unit extends to tenant consultation and environmental improvement schemes on about 50 local authority housing estates throughout England and Wales. They are listed in a NACRO briefing paper, *Neighbourhood approaches to crime prevention*, which also describes how NACRO's consultative approach works. Further information from NACRO. See also The Safe Neighbourhoods Unit.

Parliamentary All Party Penal Affairs Group. The Group's report, *The prevention of crime among young people*, describes several community policing schemes, as well as providing a comprehensive review of different approaches to crime prevention. Published by Barry Rose.

Police Review. Special policing schemes are sometimes featured in this weekly publication for the police service. From mid-1984, a quarterly insert, *Crime Prevention and Security News* is issued with *Police Review*. It contains information on commercially available security devices and on force projects and is available from T.G. Scott, 30–32 Southampton Street, London WC2E 7HR.

Police Staff College, Bramshill House, Nr Basingstoke, Hampshire, RG27 0JW. Under the College's rolling programme, police officers are encouraged to analyse problems in their own forces, with a view to bringing about and evaluating specified programmes of organisational change. Relevant papers are lodged with the College's Department of Police Management Studies.

Officers attending the College's special course and the command courses (junior, intermediate and senior) also undertake short research projects. A list of projects can be obtained from respective course directors.

The Safe Neighbourhoods Unit, 723 Commercial Road, London E14 7LD. A NACRO offshoot, the Unit is involved in tenant consultation and neighbourhood improvement schemes on twelve London housing estates. Its work is described in *The Safe Neighbourhoods Unit*, by Jon Bright and Geraldine Petterson, published by NACRO.

Tavistock Institute of Human Relations, crime and environment programme. The Institute has a small staff engaged on research on crime prevention and the environment. Part of its remit is to document successful initiatives. Further information from Barry Poyner, The Tavistock Institute of Human Relations, Belsize Lane, London NW3 5BA.

REFERENCES

Alderson, J. (1979) *Policing freedom*, Macdonald and Evans, Plymouth

Allatt, P. (1984a) 'Residential security: containment and displacement of burglary', *The Howard Journal of Criminal Justice*, vol. 23, no. 2

—— (1984b) 'Fear of crime: the effect of improved residential security on a difficult to let estate', *The Howard Journal of Criminal Justice*, vol. 23, no. 3

Association of Chief Police Officers (1979) *Report of a working party appointed by the Association of Chief Police Officers on the role of the Home Office Crime Prevention Centre* — Stafford, unpublished

Baldwin, R. and Kinsey, R. (1982) *Police powers and politics*, Quartet Books, London

Beckett, I. and Hart, J. (1981) *Neighbourhood policing*, Metropolitan Police A2(3) Branch, unpublished paper

Blaber, A. (1979) *The Exeter Community Policing Consultative Group*, NACRO, London

Bond, K. (1982) 'West Midlands Police resource experiments', in Males, S.J. (ed.), *Initiatives in police management*, Police Research Services Unit, Home Office

Bright, J.A. (1969) *The beat patrol experiment*, Police Research and Development Branch Report 8/69, Home Office, London

Bright, J. and Petterson, G. (1984) *The Safe Neighbourhoods Unit*, NACRO, London

Brown, J. (1981) *The Skelmersdale coordinated police experiment*, Cranfield Institute of Technology, Department of Social Policy

Butler, A.J.P. (1984) *Police management*, Gower, Farnborough

—— and Tharme, K. (1983) *Chelmsley Wood policing experiment*, Management Services Department, West Midlands Police, unpublished report

Cheshire Constabulary (undated), *Home watch*

Christian, Chief Superintendent (1983) *Planned policing*, paper presented to the Merseyside Police Committee, September 1983

Christian, J.D. (1982) *A planning, programming, budgeting system in the police service in England and Wales between 1969 and 1974*, MA thesis, Faculty of Economics and Social Studies, University of Manchester

Clarke, R.V.G. and Mayhew, P. (1980) *Designing out crime*, HMSO, London

—— and Hough, M. (1984) *Crime and police effectiveness*, Home Office Research Study no. 79, HMSO, London

Clifton, R. (1984) *Neighbourhood watch: problems and opportunities*, paper prepared for Community/Police Consultative Group for Lambeth, 18 September

Collins, K. (1985) 'Some issues in police effectiveness and efficiency', *Policing*, vol. 1, no. 2

Community/Police Consultative Group for Lambeth (1984) *Visiting Lambeth police stations. First report of the panel of lay visitors*

Comrie, M.D. and Kings, E.J. (1975) *Study of urban workloads*, Police Research Services Unit Report No 11/75, Home Office, London

Crime Prevention News, quarterly publication, Home Office, London

Critchley, T.A. (1978) *A history of police in England and Wales*, Constable, London

Department of Education and Science (1982) *Study of HM Inspectorate in England and Wales*, HMSO, London

Department of the Environment (1982) *Priority Estates Project 1982. Improving problem council estates: a summary of aims and progress*, London

Dix, M.C. and Layzell, A.D (1983) *Road users and the police*, Croom Helm, Beckenham

Ekblom, P. and Heal, K. (1982) *The police response to calls from the public*, Research and Planning Unit Paper 9, Home Office, London

Gladstone, F.J. (1980) *Coordinating crime prevention efforts*, Home Office Research Study No 62, HMSO, London

Goldstein, H. (1979) 'Improving policing: a problem-oriented approach', *Crime & Delinquency*, April, 236–58

———— and Susmilch, C.E. (1981a) Volume I. *The problem-oriented approach to improving police service. A description of the project and an elaboration of the concept*, University of Wisconsin Law School

———— (1981b) Volume II. *The drinking-driver in Madison. A study of the problem and the community's response*, University of Wisconsin Law School

———— (1982a) Volume III. *The repeat sexual offender in Madison. A memorandum on the problem and the community's response*, University of Wisconsin Law School

———— (1982b) Volume IV. *Experimenting with the problem-oriented approach to improving police service. A report and some reflections on the two case studies*, University of Wisconsin Law School

Greater London Council (1983a) *Home Office draft circular on crime prevention — a response*

———— (1983b) *In-depth review. Improvements to multi-storey blocks*, Report to Policy and Performance Review Committee (7 PPR 68)

Gregory, E. (1967) *Unit beat policing. Reflections on the experiments and implications of the widespread adoption of the system*, Police Research and Planning Branch Report 11/67, Home Office, London

———— and Turner, E.P. (1967) 'Unit beat policing. A new system of patrol', *Police Research Bulletin*, no. 1

Hall, A.S. (1981) *Strategies against vandalism* MSc thesis, Cranfield Institute of Technology, Department of Social Policy

Hampshire Constabulary (1981) *The Havant policing scheme*, Chief Constable's Office, unpublished report. Also reported in Males, S.J. (ed.), 1982

Hedges, A., Blaber, A. and Mostyn, B. (1980) *Community planning project. Cunningham Road Improvement Scheme*, Barry Rose, Chichester

Hibberd, M. (1984) *Neighbourhood watch. An organisational indicator*, Police Foundation, unpublished paper

HMSO (1971) *A framework for government research and development*, Cmnd 4814, London

———— (1978) *Committee of inquiry on the police. Reports on negotiating machinery and pay* (Edmund Davies Committee) Cmnd. 7283, London

———— (1982) *Efficiency and effectiveness in the civil service. Government observations on the Third Report from the Treasury and Civil Service Committee, session 1981–82*, HC 236, Cmnd 8616, London

———— (1983) *Financial management in government departments*, Cmnd 9058, London

———— (1984) *Progress in financial management in government departments*, Cmnd 9297, London

Holdaway, S. (1984) *Inside the British police*, Blackwell, Oxford

Home Office (1965) *Report of the Committee on the Prevention and Detection of Crime* (Cornish Committee)

———— (1967a) *Circular No 142/1967. Equipment for new systems of policing*

———— (1967b) *Police manpower, equipment and efficiency. Reports of three working parties*, HMSO, London

———— (1967c) *Report of Her Majesty's Chief Inspector of Constabulary for the year 1966*, HMSO, London

———— (1968a) *Crime prevention. The Home Office Standing Committee on Crime Prevention*, unnumbered circular dated 17 May

———— (1968b) *Report of Her Majesty's Chief Inspector of Constabulary for the year 1967*, HMSO, London

———— (1971) *Circular No 48/1971. Crime prevention panels*

———— (1976) *Report of the Working Group on Crime Prevention*, unpublished

—————— (1978a) *The role of crime prevention panels*, unnumbered circular dated 5 April
—————— (1978b) *Circular 211/1978. Juveniles. Cooperation between the police and other agencies.* Jointly issued with Department of Health and Social Security, Department of Education and Science and Welsh Office
—————— (1980) *Circular No 83/198. Juveniles. Cooperation between the police and other agencies*
—————— (1983a) *Community and race relations training for the police*, Report of the Police Training Council Working Party, Home Office, London
—————— (1983b) *Police probationer training*, Report of the Police Training Council Working Party, Home Office, London
—————— (1983c) *Circular No 114/1983. Manpower, effectiveness and efficiency in the police service*
—————— (1983d) *Crime reduction. Report of an interdepartmental group on crime*
—————— (1983e) *Crime prevention: a coordinated approach*, Proceedings of a seminar on crime prevention, Police Staff College, Bramshill House, 26–29 September 1982, London
—————— (1984a) *Circular 8/1984. Crime prevention*, issued jointly with Department of Education and Science, Department of Environment, Department of Health and Social Security and Welsh Office
—————— (1984b) *Criminal justice. A working paper*, London
Home Office Crime Prevention Centre (1983) *The Crime Prevention Centre*, unpublished paper
Home Office Research and Planning Unit (1984) *Research Programme*, London
Hope, T. (1982) *Burglary in schools: the prospects for prevention*, Research and Planning Unit Paper 11, Home Office, London
—————— (1985) *Implementing crime prevention measures*, Home Office Research Study No. 86, HMSO, London
—————— and Murphy, D.J.I. (1983) 'Problems of implementing crime prevention: the experience of a demonstration project', *The Howard Journal*, vol. XXII, 38–50
Hough, J.M. (1980) *Uniformed police work and management technology*, Research Unit Paper 1, Home Office, London
—————— and Mayhew, P. (1983) *The British Crime Survey: first report*, Home Office Research Study No 76, HMSO, London
Humberside Police (1981) *The Grange Project evaluation report, July 1981*, Research Services Department
—————— (undated) *The Grange Project. An experiment in community team-work*, Report for 1979–1982
Jefferson, T. and Grimshaw, R. (1984) *Controlling the constable. Police accountability in England and Wales*, Cobden Trust, London
Jones, J.M. (1980) *Organisational aspects of police behaviour*, Gower, Farnborough
Kettle, M. and Hodges, L. (1982) *Uprising! The police, the people and the riots in Britain's cities*, Pan Books, London
Laugharne, A. (1982) 'Skelmersdale coordinated policing experiment' in Males, S.J. (ed.), *Initiatives in police management*, Police Research Services Unit, Home Office, London
Libertarian Research and Education Trust (1984a) *The background to neighbourhood watch*, Working Paper No 1, London
—————— (1984b) *Community crime prevention and police attitudes towards the community*, Working Paper No 2, London
—————— (1984c) *Neighbourhood watch and crime*, Working Paper No 3, London
—————— (1984d) *Police evaluations of neighbourhood watch*, Working Paper No 4, London
Lubans, V.A. and Edgar, J.M. (1979) *Policing by objectives*, Social Development Corporation, Hartford
Maguire, M. and Bennett, T. (1982) *Burglary in a dwelling. The offence, the offender and the victim*, Heinemann, London

Males, S.J. (1982a) 'Some suggestions on how to assess the effectiveness of a policing system' in Males, S.J. (ed.), *Initiatives in police management*, Police Research Services Unit, Home Office, London

Males, S.J. (1982b) *Initiatives in police management*, Police Research Services Unit, Home Office, London

Manwaring-White, S. (1983) *The policing revolution. Police technology, democracy and liberty in Britain*, Harvester Press, Brighton

Mayhew, P. (1985) 'Target-hardening: how much of an answer?' in Clarke, R. and Hope, T. (eds.) *Coping with burglary. Research perspectives on policy*, Kluwer-Nijhoff, Boston

Metropolitan Police (1984) *A discussion document on crime prevention officers*, internal report

Moore, C. (1978) *From crime statistics to social policies*, paper to Cranfield conference on the prevention of crime in Europe, April 1978, Devon and Cornwall Constabulary
——— and Brown, J. (1981) *Community versus crime*, Bedford Square Press, London

Morris, P. and Heal, K. (1981) *Crime control and the police: a review of research*, Home Office Research Study No 67, HMSO, London

NACRO (1984) *Neighbourhood approaches to crime prevention*, NACRO Briefing, London

Northumbria Police (undated) *Prevention of fear. Part I Felling*

Openshaw, G. (1981) 'The Police Research Services Unit — its role in police research and development', *Police Research Bulletin*, no. 37 Autumn 1981, 19–21

Parliamentary All-Party Penal Affairs Group (1983) *The prevention of crime among young people*, Barry Rose, Chichester

Pearson, G. (1983) *Hooligan. A history of respectable fears*, Macmillan, London

Philips, Sir C. (1979) *In the office of chairman . . .*, James Smart Lecture

Police (1984) Training team research team appointed, vol. XVI, no. 7, p. 9

Police Review, (1983) Guidelines on lay visitors, 15 July, 1326–7

Police Staff College (1984) *Research specialism in Northumbria Police*, paper prepared for the 57th intermediate command course, Bramshill

Pope, D. (1976) *Community relations — the police response*, Runnymede Trust, London

Poyner, B. (1981) 'Crime prevention and the environment. Street attacks in city centres', *Police Research Bulletin*, no. 37

Ramsay, M. (1982) *City centre crime: the scope for situational prevention*, Research and Planning Unit Paper 10, Home Office, London

Report of the Commissioner of Police of the Metropolis for the year 1982 (1983) Cmnd 8928, HMSO, London

Report of the Commissioner of Police of the Metropolis for the year 1983 (1984) Cmnd 9268, HMSO, London

Research and Planning Unit (1984) *Research Programme, 1984–85*, Home Office, London

Riley, D. and Mayhew, P. (1980) *Crime prevention publicity: an assessment*, Home Office Research Study No 63, HMSO, London

Royal Commission on the Police (1962) *Final report*, Cmnd 1728, HMSO, London

Ryan, P.J. (1980/81) 'Home Office information service to police forces', *Police Research Bulletin*, nos. 35 and 36, Autumn 1980/Spring 1981

Ryan, P.J. and Wheatley, J. (1980/81) 'A computerised database of police research information'. *Police Research Bulletin*, nos. 35 and 36, Autumn 1980/Spring 1981

St Johnson, E. (1978) *One policeman's story*, Barry Rose, Chichester

Schaffer, E.B. (1980) *Community policing*, Croom Helm, London

Scientific Research and Development Branch (1984a), *Police Research Programme 1984/85* Home Office, London
——— (1984b) *Report on a method for evaluating policing experiments and its applica tion. The experiment at Chelmsley Wood, a sub-division of West Midlands Police*, Home Office, London

Sinclair, I. and Miller, C. (1984) *Measures of police effectiveness and efficiency*, Research and Planning Unit Paper 25, Home Office, London

Smith, D.J. (1983) *Police and people in London III: A survey of police officers*, Policy Studies Institute, London
——— and Gray, J. (1983) *Police and people in London IV: The police in action*, Policy Studies Institute, London
Smith, L.F.J. (1984) *Neighbourhood watch. A note on implementation*, Home Office, London
Softley, P., Brown, D., Forde, B., Mair, G. and Moxon, D. (1980) *Police interrogation: an observational study in four police stations*, Home Office Research Study No 61, HMSO, London
Turner, B.W.M. (1984) *Neighbourhood watch. Review of the London experience*, Paper prepared for the 59th intermediate command course, Police Staff College, Bramshill
Turner, T.P. (1966) *The use of personal radios for beat patrol*, Police Research and Planning Branch Memorandum No C9/66, Home Office, London
Veater, P. (1984) *Evaluation of Kingsdown neighbourhood watch project, Bristol, 1 March 1983–29 February 1984*, Avon and Somerset Constabulary
Wasserman, G.J. (1970) 'Planning-programming-budgeting in the police service in England and Wales', *O & M Bulletin*, November
Weatheritt, M. (1983) 'Community policing: does it work and how do we know?' in Bennett, Trevor (ed.) *The future of policing*, Cropwood Conference Series No 15, University of Cambridge
West Mercia Police (1983) *Operational support unit. Final Report*, Research and Development Department, unpublished
West Midlands Police (1982) *Resource experiments. Volume I: main report, Volume II: statistical tables*, Management Services Department, unpublished reports
Wheeler, J. (1980) *Who prevents crime?*, Conservative Political Centre, London
Williamson, F.E. (1967) 'Carlisle. A unit beat experiment', *Police Research Bulletin*, no. 2
Willis, C. (1984) *The tape-recording of police interviews with suspects*, Home Office Research Study No. 82, HMSO, London
Winchester, S. and Jackson, H. (1982) *Residential burglary: the limits of prevention*, Home Office Research Study No. 74, HMSO, London
Yates, R. (1981) *An assessment of the Skelmersdale split force coordinated policing experiment*, MSc thesis, Cranfield Institute of Technology, Department of Social Policy

INDEX